The

Marling

Menu-Master

for

ITALY

A comprehensive manual
for translating the Italian menu
into American English

By

WILLIAM E. and CLARE F. MARLING

ALTARINDA BOOKS
7455 Draper Avenue
La Jolla, CA 92037

Reprinted in 1978
Reprinted in 1979
Reprinted in 1982
Reprinted in 1984
Reprinted in 1986
Reprinted in 1990
Reprinted in 1993
Reprinted in 1996

Printed in Taiwan, R.O.C.

ISBN 0-912818-02-6

sense, although it does serve vermouths and other ape-
ritifs, beer, brandy, and different alcoholic beverages
displayed behind the bar. But, its greatest activity flows
from its CAFFÈ ESPRESSO machine. A person stops
in three or four times a day for a tiny cup of this very
strong aromatic coffee. A bar also serves made-up sand-
wiches, soft drinks, pastries, and usually ice cream and
sherbet. Many persons stop by on the way to work to have
their breakfast — a CAFFÈLATTE (half coffee and half
hot milk), or a luscious CAPPUCINO (half coffee, half
frothy steam-heated milk), and a pastry. An integral
part of many bars is the outdoor or sidewalk café with
its colorful awnings, umbrellas, tables and chairs.

EATING CUSTOMS

The food is eaten in courses, and more rigidly so in Italy
than in other countries. For example, when you order a meat
course, very likely all you will receive is a little bit of the
meat, no potatoes, no vegetables--just the meat all alone
on the plate. If you want a vegetable you must order what
you want, and it will be served on a separate dish, possibly
after your meat course, although normally it will come at
about the same time. Spaghetti, or whatever form of any
Pasta you order, is also a separate course. It is served alone,
that is, not accompanying or combined with any other food.
It will have its own sauce or other preparation, of course.

The menu (LISTA, CARTA), lists the various courses in
the order in which the Italian orders them, but, you may
select only those courses you want. You will not at all be ex-
pected to take one dish from each course. You may want
only an ANTIPASTO (appetizer), and then a fish dish (PE-
SCE), so that is all you order, thus skipping all the other
courses offered.

PANE (bread) usually is present all during the meal. It
is so much a part of the meal that the menu will list PANE
e COPERTO, the charge for the bread and the table setting.
It is as important as the knife, fork and spoon. Butter will
not be served with it.

Most bread in Italy is some variation of what we know
as French bread, a hard-crusted white bread, and it is pro-
cured daily fresh from the bakery. GRISSINI (little dry bread
sticks), also are often part of the bread offered. Normally
bread and wine will be served even before you have placed

your order. You will notice other patrons eating bits of bread and sipping wine while waiting for their first course to arrive.

BEVERAGES

COCKTAILS: There is no cocktail hour in Italy. Italians drink little hard liquor. However, at any hour during the day they may drink an APERITIVO (aperitif) such as VERMUT (vermouth, either red or white, both sweet). Vermouth is often ordered by the brand name, such as MARTINI or CINZANO, with or without GHIACCIO (ice cubes). BIRRA (beer) is also a popular drink in Italy. Except for the places catering to an elegant, international clientele, there is no provision for the making or serving of cocktails, either in a bar or café or in a restaurant. If a restaurant has a bar, you can stop by before going to your table and obtain a whisky or brandy and water, but not likely a cocktail.

COFFEE (CAFFÈ): Except for the breakfast coffee, which is mixed with hot milk (CAFFÈLATTE), coffee is not served with, or drunk during the meal. It is very strong black coffee served in tiny cups, these only half-filled, and is drunk any time during the day at a café or a bar, or after meals, with lots of ZUCCHERO (sugar) in it. It is called both CAFFÈ and simply ESPRESSO, for the elaborate machine which brews it makes only one cup at a time from each spout.

WINE (VINO): Wine is the main beverage served with meals. No attempt is being made in this little book to cover the wines of Italy, a study in itself. Nearly every small restaurant selects its own local wine by the barrel, and serves it in a carafe or other small container by the quarter, half, or full litre (a little more than a U.S. quart), both ROSSO (red) and BIANCO (white). It is reasonably priced, and you can hardly do better than to drink this wine upon which part of the reputation of the restaurant depends. Then, if you wish something a little more adventuresome, the recommendation of your waiter, from the wine list, will usually be excellent and not too expensive. The French custom when traveling, of drinking the « vin du pays », the local wine, seems an excellent one to follow, for each area usually produces not only one, but several different local wines.

WATER (ACQUA): Very popular with meals, and often mixed with the wine, is ACQUA MINERALE (mineral water). It will be a gaseous or natural spring water of one delicate taste or another. ACQUA NATURALE (plain tap water) may be drunk safely throughout Italy. The country's water purification systems seem to be very effective.

OTHER BEVERAGES (Altre Bevande, Bibite): The Italians consume quantities of soft drinks, including brand name colas familiar to us, plain or carbonated fruit juices, such as SPREMUTA d'ARANCIA (an orange-flavored drink), BIRRA (beer), and occasionally TE (tea), but rarely with a meal. It certainly would not be out of order in a restaurant to ask for a soft drink or even milk if that is what you prefer, but you will not find the Italians doing so, for they do not drink these beverages with their meals.

EATING HOURS

BREAKFAST (PRIMA COLAZIONE): 7:30–10 A.M. There is actually no breakfast in Italy as we know it. In the tourist areas, large hotels, and in those places catering to an international clientele, a breakfast may be had. In regular hotels you will receive (usually they prefer to serve it in your room) a small pot of strong Italian coffee and one of hot milk, which when mixed together become CAFFÈ-LATTE (coffee-milk), some PANE (bread), or PANINI (bread rolls), BURRO (butter), and MARMELLATA (jam). They do not serve fruit, fruit juice, or bacon and eggs, and to try to get these will cause confusion; if you are successful, it will be costly; hotels are not set up to provide breakfast, for there is no early morning kitchen staff. If you want something more substantial than what is offered, it is better to go out of the hotel and find a Rosticceria or its equivalent, where fried or scrambled eggs and bacon or ham can be ordered.

LUNCH (COLAZIONE): 12–2:30 P.M. For most Italians this is the main meal of the day. The restaurants and eating places are all set up and ready for this daily mid-day rush.

DINNER (PRANZO, CENA): 7:30–10 P.M. in the North; 8:30–10 P.M. in the Central and South. Again, the complete offerings of the restaurant will be available. Certain snack bars and short-order places will still be open for serving in the later evening.

THE ITALIAN RESTAURANT

In general, the restaurants offer a very pleasant atmosphere, whether simple or elaborate, and in the warm seasons, dining AL FRESCO (in the fresh air), is an extremely popular and a delightful custom. This can be in a courtyard, often under a grape arbor, or on a terrace, or if such is not a part of the establishment, the tables and chairs are simply put out on the sidewalk in front of the restaurant.

Restaurants are well-staffed with trained, courteous waiters; and the service is usually excellent. You need never feel rushed, for a typical meal takes time to prepare, and the management expects you to take time to enjoy it. The average Italian is accustomed to spending about 2 hours consuming a proper dinner, which is accomplished with ease and relaxation, for the bread and wine are always on the table to keep you content while waiting for a course to arrive.

Almost invariably the menu is posted outside the restaurant--in the window, or in a holder against the wall, or in the walkway leading into the restaurant. Thus you can inspect the menu, using your book for translating long before you decide to enter. Then when at the table, you can make another inspection before having to decide just what to order. You will know what is coming--no surprises! Moreover, there will be no reason for you to miss some delicious dish which you would very definitely want to try.

TIPPING

Nearly every food bill (CONTO) includes from 10-15% charge for service. This is your tip (MANCIA). But, it is customary to leave an additional amount on the table for the waiter (CAMERIERE), say 100 Lire for bills up to 1500 Lire, and from 5-7% extra for bills over 3000 Lire. At bars and snack-bars there will usually be a sign in back of the bar saying SERVIZIO COMPRESO (service included), or SERVIZIO NON COMPRESO (service not included). If service is not included, there will be a little kitty on the bar for putting in a 10-20 Lire tip.

CONFRONTING THE MENU

The menu is broken down or made up into categories of food roughly in the order in which the Italians eat them.

This book is organized to take advantage of that fact, to enable you, as rapidly as possible, to translate without having to refer back and forth.

For example, the menu will list under PESCE (fish) probably only about five or six kinds. In our fish section you will find listed alphabetically all the various fishes you are likely to encounter, and under each fish the various different methods of preparation. Thus, you should be able to untangle quickly, and understand, what is being offered in fish dishes in that restaurant, and how they are prepared. This same approach, course by course, or category by category, which may interest you, will unfold before you rapidly, all that that restaurant offers.

Different menus will call the various categories of food by different names, but this will not present a major problem as far as translating them is concerned, for they are all listed in the « Breakdown of the Menu » that follows.

Vegetables, for example, may be called CONTORNI, or VERDURE, or LEGUMI, or ORTAGGI or INSALATE, all of which refer to vegetables. Usually salads, served with meals, are listed with the vegetables.

Some menus may break down the categories of the meats into sub-headings such as Alla GRIGLIA (grilled), ARROSTI (roasted), FRITTI (fried), BOLLITI or LESSATI (boiled), but these will all be main courses, and found in this book listed alphabetically in the main course section, PIATTI del GIORNO (dishes of the day, or main courses).

The fixed price complete meal, where the restaurant offers a choice of three or four main dishes plus soup, salad or vegetable, and a modest dessert for a set price (PREZZO FISSO) is not the general custom in Italy. Therefore, if you find a main course that appeals to you, you cannot say to yourself, and certainly not to the waiter: « I think I'll have that " on the dinner " ». The closest approximation to this type of meal appears on the MENU TURISTICO (tourist menu), often printed in four different languages, and found in railway station restaurants, or in tourist areas.

PASTA

We discuss and explain PASTA (spaghetti, macaroni, ravioli, noodles) at length because it is a vital, important element in the Italian diet. Further, it has the unmistakable mark of ITALY to people the world over. When one thinks of Italian food, he immediately has visions of mountains of spaghetti, macaroni, ravioli. But, in Italy, PASTA is only one course in a meal, and is served alone, all by itself. The Italians do not have « Spaghetti Feeds » or « Spaghetti Dinners ». After PASTA come other dishes, or the main course.

WHAT IS IT?

PASTA is the general term applied to a multitude of forms of these flour-made products, such as spaghetti, macaroni, noodles, ravioli. It comes in a seemingly endless variety of shapes. Worse yet, one name in one region can be, with the same name, a different form or size in another region. The explanations in this section are as accurate as is possible, but still subject to these regional variations.

HOW IS IT MADE?

The basic ingredient of PASTA is semolina, the refined inner kernels of hard, durum wheat, ground into a semi-fine flour. It is either mixed with water, and made into a stiff dough which is turned out in hundreds of different machine-made shapes, and dried, such as spaghetti, macaroni, rigatoni, vermicelli, or, it is mixed with water and eggs, and made into a soft dough, which is tender and somewhat moist. This dough will be cut into such forms as tagliarini, fettuccini, linguini, which are flat ribbon shapes of varying widths, i.e., to us, noodles.

The third form that pasta can take is the soft dough formed into various pocket shapes such as ravioli, agnolotti, tortellini, which contain a stuffing, or flat pancakes of the dough which are stuffed and rolled.

Pasta is either white in color, or yellow when eggs are mixed into the dough, or it is green, having had cooked spinach worked into the raw dough.

FORMS OF PASTA

Apart from the PASTINA, which comes in a myriad of different tiny patterns of circles, squares, shells, stars, and is cooked and served in broth, the basic forms of pasta can roughly be divided into the following categories:

1. **Flat Ribbon (Noodles):** Tagliarini, fettuccini, linguini, tagliatelle, lasagne, etc.

2. **Solid Round Lengths:** Spaghetti, vermicelli, tonnarelli, etc.

3. **Hollow Tubes or Cylinders (Macaroni):** Bucatini, maccheroni, penne, rigatoni, etc., which are either long, or short forms.

4. **Stuffed Shapes (Ravioli):** Ravioli, agnolotti, tortellini, which are formed into small pockets which are stuffed and sealed; or cannelloni or manicotti, which are stuffed rolled sheets or large tubes of pasta.

5. **Various Other Shapes:** Conchiglie (shell), farfalle (butterfly), fusilli (spiral), orecchiette (ear-shaped), etc.

HOW IS IT PREPARED?

Pasta dishes are divided into two main categories:

PASTA or PASTINA in BRODO: Pasta cooked in, and served in broth.

PASTA ASCIUTTA (Dry Pasta): Spaghetti, ravioli, macaroni, noodles, when served as we familiarly expect them to be, that is, in a sauce of one type or another, come under this category despite the liquid sauce which is mixed through them.

These two methods of offering pasta are grouped under MINESTRE (soups, literally) on the menu, usually the PASTA in BRODO in one group, and the various preparations for PASTA ASCIUTTA in the following group.

The various forms of PASTA ASCIUTTA are cooked in boiling salted water «al Dente», that is, it is ready to serve when it reaches the point that you can bite through it with your teeth without its being mushy, and still having a tiny uncooked core in the center.

To achieve this fine point, each dish of pasta must be cooked expressly for each diner, which means a small portion at a time in a huge caldron of boiling, salted water.

It takes a great deal of experience to know when it has reached this delicate point of doneness. The pasta is then drained, and served with a sauce, and almost always topped with grated cheese; or it is boiled, drained, and then baked in the oven with a sauce and cheese.

The principal types of grated cheese sprinkled over or mixed into pasta are either PARMIGIANO (Parmesan), a slightly bitey cheese made of cow's milk, or PECORINO, a stronger, sharper cheese made of ewe's milk. The cheeses used in baked or stuffed pasta dishes such as LASAGNA

AL FORNO, mainly are MOZZARELLA, FONTINA, or RI-
COTTA, all mild, soft, white cheeses.

DEALING WITH THE MAIN COURSES

While the appetizers, soups and other first courses, plus
vegetables and desserts, are more or less straightforward
and uncomplicated, perhaps nowhere is the Italian indivi-
duality in cooking more strikingly displayed than in the preparation of the main dishes.

Not only does nearly each region have its own way of
preparing the same cut of meat, but one is convinced, from
exposure to menus, that each little district within a region
applies its own twist, and so gives its own name to a dish,
even though the difference in preparation would not be
discernible to our taste. And all this before we take into
account the person or chef preparing the dish!

PREPARATIONS VARY

Thus, no matter what a cookbook says--and even IF you
could get two cookbooks to agree on the preparation of the
same dish, which would be extremely unlikely, once a recipe
gets into the hands of the actual chef on the spot the whole
arrangement breaks down, for he will vary proportions and
ingredients to suit himself. But, it doesn't matter, for the
results are rarely disappointing.

Therefore, no extremely detailed description of a dish is
really valid. Every effort has been made to describe dishes
as accurately as possible, but be prepared for variations.
Furthermore, a dish called « alla this » one time and « alla
that » at the next restaurant is, or can be to our taste, practically the same thing.

However, certain themes do run relatively consistently.
Dishes described as « alla Marsala » will always contain
Marsala, a fortified amber wine; and veal cutlets (SCALOP-
PINE) « alla Valdostana » will have melted cheese in or on
them; « alla Milanese » will always be breaded and fried
golden, but whether in olive oil or butter is anyone's guess.

An effort has been made in listing dishes in the meat or
main dish section of this book to average out the preparation,
the main ingredients used, and especially to mention those
things that correlate a dish with its name. Thus, when you
order, you will not receive something you did not expect,
and can be reasonably certain of what it is, what is in it,
and how it is made.

A WORD ABOUT THE MEATS

The Italians cut up their animals completely differently from the way it is done, for example, in the United States. In the first place, most meat is boned. Then, instead of just cutting across the meat, the butcher strips out the natural ligaments lengthwise, and then cuts across them.

The best example, in brief, is for you to visualize a whole piece of round steak in the butcher shop at home. You will remember the several little membranes enclosing pieces of meat which can be removed whole. The Italians take out of the leg, for instance, the whole length of each of these pieces, each with its separate name, and then cut across the pieces. Thus, your round steak at home could have in it a slice each of: the GIRELLO, the CONTROGIRELLO, the SCANNELLO, the ROSA, the PICCIONE, the SOTTONOCE, the NOCE, the FESA, the CONTRONOCE, and the FRICANDO! These various cuts offered have been described in terms of American cuts.

Except in Rome, little lamb is available, and scarcely more pork. Beef is fairly common, but veal (VITELLO) is THE meat of the country. This is partly because the Italians prefer whitish meat to red, and consider tenderness rather than flavor the criterion of good meat. It is also due to a paucity of grazing land, so that cattle are eaten young, and beef are not grain fed, nor is the meat hung for aging. Much chicken, rabbit, turkey, and, when in season, wild game, including birds, are available.

BREAKDOWN OF THE MENU

ANTIPASTI: Appetizers, or first courses.
MINESTRE: Literally, soups, but in this category will be listed the following:

> **Minestre e Zuppe:** Soups.
> **Pasta in Brodo:** Pasta in soup.
> **Pasta Asciutta:** The dry pasta, as spaghetti, macaroni, noodles, with their sauces.
> **Riso, Risotto:** Rice Dishes.
> **Gnocchi:** Small dumplings served with a sauce.
> **Polenta:** A thick cornmeal mush mixture.

UOVA: Egg dishes.
PESCE e FRUTTI di MARE: Fish and seafood dishes.
PIATTI del GIORNO: Dishes of the day or main courses (meat or fowl). These may be broken down into sub-

categories. The listings vary in terminology, but they are all main courses. Some of these sub-categories are as follows:

Piatti da Farsi: Dishes that must be prepared to order.

Piatti Freddi: Cold main dishes.

Piatti Pronti: Dishes ready to serve, such as stews.

Carne: Meat.

Arrosti: Roasted meats.

Bolliti: Boiled meats.

ai **Ferri:** Grilled or broiled.

alla **Griglia:** Grilled or broiled.

Grigliate: Grilled.

Specialità della Casa: Specialty of the house.

CACCIAGIONE, SELVAGGINA: Wild game, including birds.

CONTORNI: Side dishes or vegetables, and salads served with meals. They can also be listed under any one of the following categories: **LEGUMI, INSALATE, ORTAGGI, VERDURE.**

DOLCI: Desserts (sweets).

GELATI: Ice creams, sherbets, frozen desserts.

FRUTTA: Fruit.

FORMAGGI: Cheeses.

PRACTICE MENU

At the back of your Menu-Master is a fold-out reproduction of a typical Italian menu. To gain some experience before facing your first meal in Italy, we suggest that you decipher, with the aid of your book, the dishes listed on this menu.

ANTIPASTI
(Appetizers, First Courses)

ANTIPASTI (appetizers) are the first course in a complete meal. The word means « before the pasta », and thus is a means of occupying the diner while the chef has time to prepare the spaghetti. There is a vast variety of these appetizers, and they vary with seasonal fruits and vegetables and regional basic ingredients such as seafood.

Many restaurants simply list them under ANTIPASTI ASSORTITI (assorted), or ANTIPASTI MISTI (mixed), and often present them in a display served AL CARRELLO (from a wheeled foodcart), the selection being left to the diner.

ANTIPASTI are usually cold, but hot dishes such as steamed COZZE or MUSCOLI (mussels), and occasionally such preparations as CROSTINI (sliced, fried or plain bread topped with cheese, chicken liver paste, ham or other garnish, and toasted in the oven) appear as a first course.

The most common simple ANTIPASTI ASSORTITI or MISTI are either a plate of PROSCIUTTO (thinly sliced ham), CRUDO (raw-cured ham) or COTTO (cooked ham), or a combination of sliced sausages such as SALAMI and MORTADELLA, accompanied by raw vegetables.

Cold, cooked vegetables including string beans, bell peppers, zucchini, artichokes, spinach, are also served as Antipasti. Whether served alone or combined in salads, both raw and cooked vegetables are commonly dressed with olive oil and lemon juice or vinegar.

Many types of boiled seafood such as ARAGOSTA, ASTACO (lobster), GAMBERI (shrimp), SCAMPI (prawns), COZZE or MUSCOLI (mussels) and CALAMARI (squid) are offered. They can also be shelled and combined as a cold salad with olive oil and lemon juice. They are listed under such headings as ANTIPASTI di MARE (sea), di NAVE (boat), alla MARINARA (sailor's style).

Other standard Antipasti listed separately on the menus will include ACCIUGHE (anchovies), SARDINE (sardines), CAVIALE (caviar), SALMONE (smoked or cold boiled salmon), ARROSTI (cold roast meats sliced), TONNO (tuna), various liver patés and many INSALATE (salads) of all types.

Certain methods of preparation such as all'AGRO (with oil and lemon juice or vinegar) apply to many different dishes. These are listed alphabetically in this section, along with other key words such as COTTO (cooked) or CRUDO (raw) which apply to foods offered as Antipasti.

ANTIPASTI
(Appetizers, First Courses)

ACCIUGHE (Filetto di): Anchovies (Filets of).
   al Burro: Served with butter for your bread.
ACETO: Vinegar.
   all'Aceto: With vinegar.
   sott'Aceto: Preserved in vinegar.
AFFETTATO (-I): Sliced, and usually refers to cold cuts of meat or sausage.
AFFUMICATO: Smoked.
AGLIO: Garlic.
AGRO (all'): A dressing of oil and lemon juice.
ALICI: Anchovies, cured in salt.
ANGUILLA: Eel (See under PESCE--fish).
ANTIPASTO (-I): Appetizers or first courses.
   Assortiti: Assorted sliced sausages, olives, other raw and cooked vegetables.
   alla **Buranella:** Mixed seafoods: boiled shrimp, mussels, squid, clams, with oil and lemon juice dressing.
   della **Casa:** Of the restaurant.
   di **Magro:** Assorted but without meat.
   di **Mare,** alla **Marinara:** Seafood appetizers: boiled shrimp, mussels, squid, clams, with oil and lemon juice dressing.
   Misti: Mixed or varied.
   Misto Nave: Mixed seafood appetizers, same as di Mare.
   Pesce Misto Mare: Mixed seafood appetizers, same as di Mare.
   a **Piacere:** Of your choice.
   a **Scelta:** Same as above.
ARAGOSTA: Spiny lobster, no claws, a California lobster.
ARINGA: Herring.
   e **Citrioli Russo:** Herring, cucumbers, boiled red beets, hard-boiled eggs, with thick cream or mayonnaise dressing.
ARROSTO (-I): Roasted, as cold cuts of roasted meats.
ASSORTITI: Assorted.
ASTACO: True lobster with claws, the Maine lobster, not found in the Mediterranean.
BAGNA CAUDA: (See under PIATTI del GIORNO--Main Dishes).
BOLLITO (-I): Boiled.

BOTTARGA: Tuna or mullet roe (fish eggs), pressed dry, salted and cut in pieces, dressed with oil and lemon juice.

BRESAOLA: A preserved raw beef, sliced paper thin, listed as di Chiavenna, Sondrio, Valtellina, all towns in the Lombardy region.

BURRO (al): Cooked in, or served with butter.

CALAMARI: Squid.

CALDO: Warm or hot.

CAPONATA: Diced eggplant, bell peppers, onions and tomatoes, fried in olive oil, then mixed together with herbs, olives, capers, vinegar, sugar. Served cold.

CAPPERI: Capers.

CARCIOFI: Artichokes.

CARCIOFINI: Very small, tender artichokes.

CARNE: Meat.

CARRELLO (al): From the food cart.

CASA (della): Of the restaurant.

CASALINGA (alla): Homemade, or house style.

CAVIALE: Caviar. Listed variously as Danese (Danish); Iraniano Beluga (Iranian Beluga); Malossal Beluga (Russian Beluga); del Volga (Volga River)--the roe or eggs of the Beluga, largest member of the sturgeon family.

   e **Crostini**: Caviar served on rounds of buttered toast.

   Tartino di, alla Francese: Caviar served on small rounds of buttered bread, French style.

CAVOLFIORE: Cauliflower.

CECI: Chick peas or garbanzo beans.

CETRIOLI: Cucumbers.

   sott'**Aceto**: Pickles.

CETRIOLINI sott'ACETO: Gherkins, or small pickles cured in vinegar.

CHIOCCIOLE: Snails.

CIPOLLA: Onion.

CIPOLLINE: Pearl onions.

COPPA: Similar to Canadian bacon, served cold, sliced.

COPPA di FRUTTA: Cup or goblet of fresh fruits, or fruit cocktail.

COTTO: Cooked.

COZZE: Mussels (See under PESCE--Fish).

CROCCHETTE di RISO: Rice croquettes with cheese in the center, deep-fried.

CROSTINI: Small slices of white bread, or fried white bread with any type of mixture of cheese, ham, chicken liver paste, anchovies, tomatoes, etc. The ingredients

CROSTINI: (cont.)

are put between slices of bread and skewered, or made individually with the garnish on top and then toasted in the oven.

di **Fegatini:** With a chicken liver mixture.

alla **Provatura:** With slices of cheese made from Buffalo milk. The slices of bread, with the cheese are skewered and heated in the oven, and then a mixture of melted butter and anchovies is poured over after the dish is taken from the oven.

CRUDO: Raw.

CULATELLO di PARMA: A type of prosciutto (ham) from Parma.

DOLCE: Sweet or mild, as mildly smoked.

FAGIOLI: Beans, either dry white or kidney.

con **Tonno:** Cold cooked white beans, raw sliced onions and tuna with an oil and vinegar, or oil and lemon juice dressing.

Toscani con Tonno: Same as above.

FAGIOLINI: String beans.

FARCITO (-I) (-E): Stuffed or filled.

FEGATO: Liver.

d'**Oca:** Goose liver.

di **Volatili:** Liver of various types of fowl.

FESA in GELATINA: Roasted veal round steak in aspic.

FICHI: Figs.

FILETTO (-I) (di): Filets of.

FINOCCHIO: The white, celery-like vegetable with a licorice flavor, eaten both raw and cooked.

FINOCCHIONA TOSCANA: A pure pork salami flavored with fennel, a Tuscan specialty.

FORNO (al): Baked in the oven.

FREDDO (-A): Cold, served cold.

FRITTELLE: Fritters, made with cheese, ham, cooked vegetables.

FRUTTI di MARE: Seafood.

FUNGHI (-ETTI) (-ETTINI): Mushrooms, from large to smaller sizes.

GALATINA in GELATINA: A pressed meat or chicken loaf in aspic.

di **Cappone:** Of capon.

di **Pollo:** Of chicken.

di **Prosciutto Farcita:** Stuffed with ham.

GAMBERI (-ETTI) (-ELLI) (-ONI): Shrimps and Prawns (See under PESCE--Fish).

GELATINA (con) (in): In aspic, or encased in gelatin.

GHIACCIATO: Iced or chilled.

GIRELLO: Cold round steak roast of veal sliced.

    Tonnato: Sliced, covered with a mayonnaise sauce made with mashed tuna, anchovies, and garnished with capers and lemon wedges.

GRANCHIO (-EOLA) (-EVOLA): Crab (See under PESCE--Fish).

INSALATA: Salad.

    Capricciosa: Thinly sliced or diced mixed vegetables, possibly with strips of ham or sausage added, in a mayonnaise sauce.

    di **Gamberetti:** Shrimp salad with mayonnaise dressing.

    di **Nervette:** Cold boiled calf's head cut into thin strips and combined with cooked white beans, sliced raw onions, oil and vinegar.

    di **Pesce:** Seafood salad; cold boiled seafood with oil and lemon juice dressing.

    di **Pollo:** Chicken salad with mayonnaise.

    di **Riso:** Cold boiled rice mixed with diced vegetables anchovies, seafood or tuna, with mayonnaise dressing.

    Russa: Finely diced cooked vegetables, hard-boiled eggs, mixed with mayonnaise.

    Testina: Same as Insalata di Nervette.

    Viennese: A mixture of tuna, hard-boiled eggs, onion, cooked beans, pickles, olives.

    Zampa e Testina: Boiled calf's feet and head cut in narrow strips, combined with cooked white beans, sliced raw onions, oil and vinegar.

INVOLTINI in GELATINA: Very thin slices of veal or beef stuffed, rolled, fried and then put in aspic.

LESSO (-I): Boiled.

LIMONE (con) (al): Lemon or lemon juice.

LINGUA: Tongue.

    alla **Escarlate:** Boiled, preserved tongue, sliced, and served cold.

    Salmistrata: Same as above.

    Scarlatta: Same as above.

LUMACHE: Snails.

    alla **Borgognona:** Burgundy style--stuffed with garlic and parsley butter, cooked and served in the shells. Alla Francesca, and alla Parigina are the same.

    alla **Romana:** Cooked in tomato and anchovy sauce.

MAGRO: Lean, but di Magro means without meat when applied to Antipasti.

MAIONESE (con): With mayonnaise.

MARE (di), MARINARA (alla): Of the sea (See under PESCE--Fish).

MARINATA: Marinated.

MELONE o FICHI con PROSCIUTTO: Chilled melon or figs served with raw-cured ham.

MISTO (-I): Mixed, or a variety of.

MORTADELLA: A large baloney type sausage made of pork meat with big bits of pork fat, whole peppercorns and pistacchio nuts.

MOSCARDINI: Small squid or cuttlefish.

MOSTARDA: Mustard.

MUSCOLI: Mussels (See under PESCE--Fish).

NAVE (di): From a boat, meaning fish or seafood.

NOSTRALE (NOSTRANO): Home product, home-grown or local.

OGNI TIPO (di): Of every type.

OLIO: Oil, usually olive oil.

all'**Olio:** Dressed with oil.

sott'**Olio:** Preserved in oil.

all'**Olio e Limone:** With oil and lemon juice dressing.

OLIVE: Olives.

    Nere: Black.

    Ripiene: Stuffed.

    Verde: Green.

OSTRICHE: Oysters.

PANCETTA: Bacon.

    Affumicata: Smoked bacon.

    Coppata: Thin slab of smoked, cured bacon rolled and sliced.

PARMA (di): From Parma, Emilia-Romagna region.

PATE: Liver or other meat or both, finely ground into a paste, or made into a meat loaf, sliced and served cold.

di **Fegato:** Made of liver.

di **Fegato d'Oca:** Made of goose liver.

di **Pollo Tartufato:** Made of chicken livers with truffles.

PEOCI: Venetian name for mussels (See under PESCE--Fish).

PEPE: Pepper.

PEPERONATA: Sliced bell peppers, onions, tomatoes, stewed in oil and garlic and served cold.

PEPERONCINI: A very small conical green pepper preserved in vinegar.

PEPERONI: Bell peppers, red, green or yellow.

> **Arrosti:** Roasted, then served cold with olive oil.

PESCE: Fish. Specific preparations for fish dishes served as appetizers or first courses will be found in the fish and seafood category (PESCE e FRUTTI di MARE).

PIACERE (a): Of your choice.

POLLO: Chicken.

POLPO (-I), POLIPO (-I): Octopus (See under PESCE-- Fish).

POMODORI: Tomatoes.

con **Tonno:** Tomatoes and canned tuna, dressed with olive oil and vinegar.

POMPELMO: Grapefruit.

PORCHETTA ROMANA: A whole large pig stuffed with rosemary and other herbs, roasted on a spit, then cut into large slices across the body. Eaten both hot and cold as an appetizer.

PORZIONE (a): Charged according to the portion taken.

PREZZEMOLO: Parsley.

PROSCIUTTO: Ham; comes AFFUMICATO (smoked), COTTO (cooked), or CRUDO (raw-cured). The raw-cured is the most popular preparation, and considered a great delicacy. The curing of this ham involves a salting process first, and then it is air-dried for aging. It is produced in various parts of the country, and hams from San Daniele, Langhirano and Parma are especially prized. Prosciutto is served sliced razor thin. It is also used extensively to flavor sauces and vegetables.

di **Cinghiale:** Made from wild boar.

> **Dolce:** Slightly less salted than normal raw-cured ham.

di **Praga:** From Prague in Czechoslovakia.

> **Tedesco:** Westphalian ham from Germany.

> **Tirolo:** From the Tyrol in Austria.

> **York:** Cooked ham from England.

RADICI, RAPANELLI, RAVANELLI: Radishes.

RIPIENE: Stuffed or filled.

SALAME (-I): All types of sausages made of minced pork meat that is seasoned, cured and served cold sliced. The sausage is often listed with the name of the area from which it comes.

SALAMINO: Small-sized salame.

> **Cacciatora:** Small hard dry salame.

SALE: Salt.

SALMONE: Salmon.
>   **Affumicato:** Smoked salmon.
>   **Scozzese:** From Scotland.

SALSA: Sauce.

SALSICCE: Any sausage which has to be cooked.
>   di **Cinghiale:** Wild boar sausage.

SALUMI: General term for all sausages served cold, sliced.

SARDINE: Sardines.

SCAMPI: Prawns (See under PESCE--Fish).

SCELTA (a): Of your choice.

SEDANO: Celery.

SENAPE: Mustard.

SEPPIE: Small cuttlefish (See under PESCE--Fish).

SOTTACETI: Various vegetables pickled in vinegar, and also means pickles.

SPIEDO (allo): Skewered or turned on a spit.

SPINACI: Spinach.

SUPREMA di POLLO in GELATINA: Poached chicken breast in aspic.

TARTUFI: Truffles.
>   **Bianchi:** White.
>   **Neri:** Black.

TONNO: Tuna.

TONNATO VITELLO: Cooked, sliced veal covered with a mayonnaise type sauce made with mashed tuna and anchovies and garnished with capers and lemon wedges.

UOVA alla RUSSA: Hard-boiled eggs stuffed with cooked tuna or salmon mixed with yolks and mayonnaise, and elaborately garnished.

VARIO al CARRELLO: Various appetizers from the food cart.

VENTRESCA di TONNO: Bellymeat of tuna fish--this is mostly canned.

VITELLO: Veal.
>   **Arrosto:** Cold sliced roast veal.
>   in **Salsa Tonnata:** Same as Tonnato Vitello.
>   **Tonnato:** Same as above.

VONGOLE: Clams.

ZUCCHINI: Italian squash.

MINESTRE
(Soups and Starch Courses)

Here is a marked peculiarity of the Italian menu. Strictly speaking MINESTRE means soups. However, it is under this heading that you will find the long-awaited spaghetti and noodle treats. By tradition this section or category on the menu lists the various products made from flour. The all-encompassing, general term for these products (spaghetti, macaroni, noodles, ravioli, lasagne) is PASTA. You will hear this term spoken over and over again, but will almost never find it written on the menu.

Other frequently listed flour or grain products in this category include RISO or RISOTTO (rice); GNOCCHI (small flour or potato dumplings); and in the North, POLENTA (a thick cornmeal mush). The various preparations for both GNOCCHI and POLENTA are listed in the section titled PASTA.

MINESTRE e ZUPPE
(Soups)

Italian soup, MINESTRA or ZUPPA can be a light course in a meal, or a heavy, hearty meal in itself if it is MINESTRONE (a thick vegetable soup, usually with rice or pasta in it), or ZUPPA di PESCE (made with various fish and seafood).

MINESTRINA (a thin clear broth) is made of either MANZO (beef) or POLLO (chicken) stock. When various forms of PASTA or PASTINA (very small shapes of pasta) are added, it becomes PASTA in BRODO.

There are also clear consommes, which when boiled down to make them stronger are referred to as RISTRETTO (reduced), or DOPPIO (double strength). If a puff pastry shell is added as a garnish it is called CONSOMME REALE (royal); if beaten eggs are strung into it, it is STRACCIA-TELLA: or if a whole poached egg on a piece of fried bread is added, it is PAVESE.

The famous MINESTRONE, which can also be served cold, is prepared differently in each region, and most certainly by each chef, but it is basically a thick soup made of combinations of vegetables and seasonings with pasta or rice added.

A variety of pureed vegetable soups, such as CREMA di ASPARAGI (cream of asparagus), FUNGHI (mushrooms),

PISELLI (peas), or POMODORO (tomato) are offered. Certain soups are served with CROSTINI (toasted bread croutons or fried bread) either in the soup or separately.

MINESTRE E ZUPPE
(Soups)

BRODO: Broth or bouillon.

> **Liscio:** Plain, simple broth.

di **Manzo:** Beef broth.

di **Pollo:** Chicken broth.

BRODO (In): Cooked and served in broth.

> **Canederli:** A tennis ball size dumpling made with seasoned bread, moistened and mixed with diced smoked bacon.

> **Capelletti:** Little button-like discs of pasta.

> **Capelli d'Angelo:** Angel's hair - - a very, very fine spaghetti.

con **Fegatini:** With chicken livers.

alla **Giardiniera:** Rice with garden vegetables cut in very small pieces.

> **Pasta, Pastina:** Various small and very small shapes of pasta.

con **Piselli:** Rice with peas.

> **Quadretti (-ini) (-ucci):** Small to very small squares of pasta.

> **Ravioli (-ini):** Stuffed small pockets of pasta.

> **Riso:** Rice.

> **Taglielini, Taglierini, Taglioline:** Narrow to very narrow noodles.

> **Tortellini:** Little, round, doughnut-shaped stuffed pasta.

e **Verdura:** Rice with chopped greens.

BRODETTO: A fish soup made of various fish and/or seafood, onions, garlic, herbs, tomatoes, white wine or vinegar, and possibly with saffron.

di **Pesce:** Same as Brodetto.

BURRIDA: A fish soup made with variety of fish cut in pieces and/or shellfish, cooked with onion, garlic, carrots, celery, anchovies, tomatoes, dried mushrooms, chopped parsley. A cross between a soup and a stew.

BUSECCA: A thick soup made with tripe, vegetables, seasonings.

27

CACCIUCCO: A fish soup made with a variety of fish and seafood, tomatoes, red wine, and served with garlic-flavored croutons.

CONSOMME: Consomme.

Doppio: Double strength, made by boiling down broth.

Gelee: Jellied consomme.

Julienne: With small strips of root vegetables.

Madrilena: Flavored with tomato juice.

con **Passatelli:** With very small forms of pasta made with flour, egg, Parmesan cheese, grated bread, which is forced through a coarse sieve.

con **Pastina:** With very small shapes of various forms of pasta.

Reale: Royal - - chicken consomme with garnish of small puff pastry shells.

Ristretto: Reduced or strengthened broth.

di **Tartaruga:** Turtle soup.

COZZE alla MARINARA: Mussels cooked in a broth (See under PESCE - - fish).

CREMA: Cream soup.

d'**Asparagi:** Cream of asparagus.

di **Funghi:** Cream of mushroom.

di **Piselli:** Cream of pea.

di **Pomodoro:** Cream of tomato.

di **Verdura:** Cream of vegetable.

CUSCUSU di TRAPANI: From Sicily, basically a variation of the Arab « Couscous », cracked wheat, water steamed, served in a fish soup containing pieces of boiled fish.

FREDDA: Served cold.

MINESTRA: Soup.

in **Brodo:** Pasta or rice cooked in broth.

di **Castagne:** Chestnut soup.

di **Ceci:** Made with garbanzo beans (chickpeas).

d'**Erbe Maritata:** Soup containing bits of meat, chopped greens such as chickory, escarole, lettuce, romaine.

di **Fagioli:** Dried bean soup.

di **Funghi:** Mushroom soup.

di **Lenticchie:** Lentil soup.

di **Pasta e Ceci:** With pasta and garbanzo beans (chickpeas).

di **Pomodoro:** Tomato soup.

MINESTRINA: Thin, clear soup - - a broth.

MINESTRONE: Any of a variety of vegetable soups, rather thick with mixed vegetables with added rice, barley or small pasta. It will vary according to the region and the chef.

alla **Casalinga:** Homemade, or in home-style.

alla **Fiorentina:** Florence style - - made with white beans in it.

alla **Genovese:** Genoa style - - with fresh basil in it.

all'**Italiana:** With mixed vegetables, but also with fresh pork rind and chopped ham.

alla **Milanese:** Milan style - - mixed vegetables, but including chopped cabbage, bacon, garlic, sage, rosemary, bay leaf, and rice.

di **Pasta:** With pasta in it.

al **Pesto:** With mixed vegetable, mushrooms, olive oil, flavored with a paste of mashed fresh basil, garlic, olive oil and Pecorino or Parmesan cheese.

alla **Piemontese:** Piedmont style - - mixed vegetables with mushrooms, often a touch of truffle and some rice or pasta.

di **Riso:** With rice in it.

Semifreddo: With rice, served cold.

alla **Toscana:** Tuscany style - - with dried white beans, chopped ham, rosemary.

e **Verdura:** With rice and chopped green vegetables.

MUSCOLI alla MARINARA: Mussels cooked in a broth (See under PESCE - - fish).

PASSATE di LEGUMI: Puree of vegetables.

PASSATELLI alla BOLOGNESE: Bologna style - - Fresh pasta made with eggs, breadcrumbs, Parmesan cheese, passed through a coarse sieve, and cooked in broth.

PESCE: Fish. For specific preparations consult the main category of PESCE e FRUTTI di MARE (Fish and Seafoods).

RISI e BISI: Rice cooked in broth with fresh peas, flavored with onions, chopped ham or bacon, seasonings.

RISI e CECI: Rice and garbanzo beans (chickpeas) cooked in broth and tomato flavored.

STRACCIATELLA: A soup similar in appearance to Chinese Egg Flower soup - - eggs, flour, grated Parmesan cheese lightly beaten and then poured into hot broth and stirred.

alla **Romana:** Roman style - - same as above, but possibly with only beaten egg yolks, or with a little lemon juice in the egg, flour, cheese mixture that is poured into the hot broth.

TAZZA (In): In a cup.

ZUPPA: Another name for soup, more earthy than Minestra.

di **Castagne:** Chestnut soup.

di **Ceci:** Of garbanzo beans (chickpeas).

Certosina, or di Verdura alla: Made by simmering small fish, onion, parsley, celery, olive oil, tomato paste in water to make a broth, which is then strained, and into it folded a lightly beaten egg with grated Parmesan cheese.

di **Cipolle:** Onion soup.

alla **Coda di Bue:** Oxtail soup.

alla **Coltivatore:** Farmer style - - with vegetables and chopped smoked bacon.

alla **Contadina:** Peasant style - - with mixed vegetables, garlic, bay leaf, red wine, rice.

di **Cozze:** Mussel soup or chowder.

di **Datteri:** Soup made from a mussel with a shell shaped like a date.

di **Fagioli:** Made with dried beans.

di **Frutti di Mare:** Made with various kinds of seafood,

di **Funghi:** Of fresh or dried mushrooms.

Julienne: A soup with finely cut strips of various vegetables in it.

di **Muscoli:** Mussel soup or chowder.

di **Ortaggi:** Of greens and other vegetables.

alla **Paesana:** Peasant style - - a vegetable soup with herbs, chopped anchovies, grated Parmesan cheese.

Pavese all'Uovo: Slices of toasted French bread topped with a raw egg, sprinkled with grated Parmesan cheese, hot broth poured over, and all browned in the oven.

di **Peoci:** Another name for mussels (See under PESCE-fish).

di **Pesce:** Fish soup. Can be any mixture of fish and/ or seafood, vegetables, herbs.

di **Pollo:** Chicken soup.

di **Primavera:** Springtime soup - - with mixed fresh garden vegetables.

Reale: Royal soup - - a consomme garnished with a puff pastry floated on top, or a pasta-dumpling made with various vegetable essences and egg.

Santé: With puree of potatoes and sorrel leaves - - an herb.

di **Sedano:** Celery soup.

ZUPPA: (cont.)

di **Trippa (e):** Tripe (beef stomach lining) soup with herbs, tomatoes, and other seasonings.

di **Verdura:** Of greens and other finely chopped vegetables.

di **Vongole:** Of clams, a clam chowder.

RISO, RISOTTO
(Rice Dishes)

Basically RISO is a word for uncooked grains of rice, but in food preparations, it is used interchangeably with RISOTTO, the word for cooked rice. While pasta is the universal starch throughout Italy, rice may act as a substitute for it, especially in the North, and is served the same way, that is, as one separate course in a meal.

Usually it is cooked with one or more vegetables, peas, sliced mushrooms or asparagus, often with bits of chicken liver, chopped meat, seafood or herbs, cooked in a broth. Be prepared to be served rice that is not completely cooked through, for this is the custom in Italy.

Since grated cheese, mostly PARMIGIANO, is almost invariably either mixed through the rice dish or sprinkled on top, we do not repeat this ingredient for all the various rice dishes listed in this section.

RISO, RISOTTO
(Rice Dishes)

RISO: Rice.

Arancino di, alla Siciliana: Orange-sized ball of cooked rice stuffed with seasoned chopped meat, breaded and fried.

al **Burro:** Sautéed in butter, onion and possibly beef marrow, cooked with added broth and served with more butter mixed through.

al **Burro con Piselli:** With butter and peas - - sautéed in butter, onion, and cooked with fresh peas in added meat broth.

in **Cagnone:** Simply boiled rice served topped with grated Parmesan cheese and browned butter flavored with garlic and sage.

RISO: (cont.)

con **Fagioli:** With dried beans - - sautéed in butter and onion, and cooked in added broth; served with cooked dried beans mixed through.

con **Funghi:** With mushrooms - - sautéed in butter; when half-cooked, rice that has been boiled in water is added to a sauce of the sautéed mushrooms, tomato paste, onion, carrot, parsley, celery, garlic and olive oil.

alla **Greca:** Greek - - can either be a pilaf (cooked in broth), then mixed with cooked vegetables and sausage, or cooked in meat broth, and when still hot is mixed with beaten egg yolks flavored with lemon juice.

Mantecato: Sautéed in butter, cooked in milk.

alla **Pescatora:** Fisherman's style - - cooked in fish broth and served with pieces of sautéed fish and/or seafood mixed through.

al **Pomodoro:** With tomatoes - - cooked with, or in tomato sauce.

Risi e Bisi: Rice and peas, a Venetian dish - - sautéed in butter with chopped onion, bacon, and cooked in broth with fresh peas.

Risi e Ceci: Rice and chickpeas cooked with tomato sauce.

Sartu di: A Naples dish. A baked, molded preparation with a breadcrumb crust, filled with layers of rice cooked in a sauce, and interspersed with a mixture of chicken livers, meat balls, mushrooms, sausage, peas, and both a tomato meat sauce and a creamed white one and topped with grated cheese.

al **Sugo:** In a meat sauce - - boiled rice finished cooking in an herbal, tomato meat sauce.

alle **Vongole:** With clams - - onion, garlic, leek, with or without tomato, sautéed in olive oil, then steamed clams added, then rice sautéed in this sauce and cooked with added broth.

alle **Vongole in Bianco:** Same as above without tomatoes.

RISOTTO: Rice.

con **Asparagi:** Cooked in broth with chopped asparagus, bacon, and onions sautéed in butter.

Bianco con Fegatini: Rice cooked in broth and white wine with sautéed chicken livers.

alla **Bolognese:** Cooked in a sauce of finely chopped beef, bacon, tomatoes, onions, garlic, basil, parsley, to which broth is added.

RISOTTO: (cont.)

alla **Campagnola:** Cooked in a sauce of tomato paste, bacon, carrot, garlic, parsley, onion, to which broth is added, then sautéed mushrooms.

alla **Certosina:** Cooked in a fish and prawn stock, and served with pieces of prawn and shrimp mixed through.

alla **Finanziera:** Sautéed in butter, brandy and chopped bacon, to which meat broth is added, finally sautéed chicken livers added.

con **Frutti di Mare:** With seafood - - sautéed in oil and butter, white wine, onion, small pieces of several seafoods such as prawns, shrimps, squid, and cooked in a broth made from boiling the seafood.

con **Funghi:** Sautéed in butter, onion, white wine, beef marrow and fresh and dried mushrooms, to which broth is added. May also have tomato in it.

alla **Genovese:** Semi-cooked rice added to sautéed onion, mushrooms and tomatoes, and cooked with added water.

Mantecato con Funghi: Sautéed in butter with mushrooms to which milk is added for the final cooking.

alla **Marinara:** Sautéed with onions, garlic in butter and olive oil, with tomato sauce; then cooked in added broth from the steamed clams and boiled prawns which are added to the mixture together with small squid when the rice is cooked, and mixed through it.

alla **Milanese:** Sautéed in butter with onion, white wine, and beef marrow, then cooked in added broth with some saffron, and finished with butter mixed through.

alla **Parmigiana:** Cooked in meat broth with chicken livers, sausage, mushrooms, tomato paste, lard, onion, carrot, celery.

di **Peoci alla Veneta:** Sautéed in butter and olive oil, cooked in added broth, then having steamed mussels and their broth mixed through.

Pescatore: Fisherman's style - - cooked in fish broth with pieces of sautéed fish and/or seafood mixed through.

a **Piacere:** To your order, as you wish it cooked.

alla **Piemontese:** Simply boiled in meat stock, and when nearly done grated Parmesan cheese and butter mixed through, with a touch of nutmeg. Served with thin meat gravy or roast juices on top, and can also have sliced white truffle.

con **Piselli:** Rice and fresh peas cooked together, and then mixed into a sauce of onion, bacon, chopped meat sautéed in butter.

RISOTTO: (cont.)

con **Quaglie:** Rice sautéed in butter and chopped onion, cooked in added broth, served under quail sautéed in olive oil, white wine, and flavored inside with sage and rosemary.

con **Rigaglie:** With chicken giblets. Cooked with giblets and veal sautéed in a sauce of beef marrow, white wine, tomato, with added meat broth.

con **Seppie:** Sliced small cuttlefish sautéed in olive oil, onion, red wine, garlic, tomato paste, to which rice is added together with boiling water to finish the cooking.

alla **Valenciana:** This is the Spanish Paella. To a broth are added separately sautéed pieces of pork, veal, Chorizo sausage, steamed clams in their shells, sautéed squid, tomatoes, red bell pepper, garlic, onion, saffron, crab, bay leaf, and all simmered together. This broth is poured over oil-sautéed raw rice, and then cooked with all the meats mixed through. There are variations in the ingredients.

alla **Veneta:** With mussels. Sautéed in butter, garlic, onion, and cooked in added juice from steaming the mussels, a fish broth. Served with the mussels mixed through.

alle **Vongole:** Onion, garlic, leek, sautéed in olive oil; then steamed clams added, then rice sautéed in this sauce and cooked with added clam broth.

SUPPLÌ: Rice balls with a center of Mozzarella cheese, poached in broth, or dipped in egg batter, breaded and deep-fried.

FORMS of PASTA
and
PASTA SAUCES and SPECIAL PREPARATIONS

In this section you will find:

1. **DESCRIPTIONS OF THE VARIOUS TYPES OR FORMS OF PASTA NORMALLY FOUND ON MENUS.**

2. **SPECIFIC PREPARATIONS APPLIED TO CERTAIN TYPES OF PASTA,** such as « Cannelloni alla Partenopea », or « Ravioli alla Genovese », which are listed directly under the type of pasta involved.

3. **SAUCES AND PREPARATIONS WHICH ARE USED INTERCHANGEABLY WITH VARIOUS TYPES OF PASTA,** such as « alla Bolognese », « alla Carbonara », and nearly sixty others, which would be the same sauce or treatment whether on spaghetti, on fettuccine, or on taglierini, or on trenette, or on other types.

alla **ABRUZZESE:** Abruzzi style; a sauce with oil, garlic, and bell peppers.

con **ACCIUGHE:** A sauce with mashed anchovies, garlic, olive oil and parsley, with or without tomatoes.

con **AGLIO E OLIO:** Served with olive oil in which garlic has been simmered.

AGNOLOTTI: A round or semi-round meat-stuffed pasta; a round ravioli.

alla **Piemontese:** Served in a mild brown meat sauce.

alla **AMATRICIANA:** In a sauce of diced bacon, olive oil, garlic, tomato, red peppers and onion.

alla **ARRABBIATA (ICA):** A tomato herbal sauce with cayenne pepper, bits of spicy sausage and bacon.

BAVETTI: A fairly thin, flat noodle.

alla **BESCIAMELLA:** A standard creamed white sauce of butter, flour and milk; usually poured over boiled pasta, then oven-browned.

BIGOLI: If in Venice area, is a round, solid pasta (a spaghetti). If elsewhere, may be a very small diameter, long tubular pasta (a macaroni).

alla **BOLOGNESE:** This is the classical meat sauce Americans associate with spaghetti; of ground meat, bacon, garlic, onion, herbs, tomato, olive oil, carrot, celery; the vegetables being very finely minced. Also called al RAGU, and al SUGO.

PASTA: (cont.)

alla **BOSCAIOLA:** Woodman's style; a sauce of mashed canned tuna and anchovy, tomato, olive oil, parsley, mushrooms and garlic.

alla **BUCANIERA:** A sauce of olive oil, garlic, tomatoes, parsley and diced octopus, lobster tail and clams.

al **BURRO:** The pasta is mixed with fresh butter, and usually also grated Parmesan cheese.

alla **CACCIATORA:** Hunter's style; usually means in an herbal tomato-meat sauce with mushrooms, white wine, and other seasonings.

con **CACIO e PEPE:** With black pepper and a cheese which becomes stringy when mixed into the hot pasta.

CALZONE: A sort of sheet-pasta turnover, stuffed with cheese, ham, salami, and baked in the oven.

alla **CAMPAGNOLA:** Sauce of mushrooms, tomatoes, olive oil, garlic, parsley, rosemary, butter.

CANEDERLI: A tennis-ball size dumpling made with moistened bread, and having smoked bacon diced in it; served with a tomato-based sauce.

CANNELLONI: When home-made is of a sheet of pasta rolled around a stuffing making a filled cylinder 3"-4" long; served baked and covered with a sauce and cheese. When machine-made is a smooth or ridged tube stuffed, and served in same way. Stuffing is herbs, meats, cheese.

alla **Partenopea:** Poetic name for Naples (style); stuffed with a mixture of Ricotta (a type of cottage cheese), and Mozzarella cheese, chopped ham, eggs, and baked in a sauce of tomato, chopped basil, grated Parmesan, and butter.

alla **Romagnola:** Romagna area style; meat-mixture stuffed, and baked in a sauce flavored with garlic and parsley.

CANNOLO (I): Short, cut lengths of macaroni (tubes).

CAPPELLETTI: Round, cap-shaped, either stuffed as a ravioli, or non-stuffed.

alla **Romagnola:** Stuffed with mixture of Ricotta cheese, roast pork loin, chicken breast, nutmeg; served with a meat sauce.

CAPPELLINI: A long, very thin diameter spaghetti.

alla **CARBONARA:** Coal dealer's style; in a sauce of diced bacon simmered in olive oil and butter with garlic.

PASTA: (cont.)

alla **CARBONARA:** (cont.)

Hot, boiled spaghetti or other pasta is poured over beaten egg yolks and mixed together; then sauce mixed through, and grated cheese sprinkled over.

alla **CARRATTIERA:** In a sauce of canned tuna, garlic, oil, diced hog jowels, mushrooms and meat sauce.

della **CASA:** Style of that particular house or restaurant; could be nearly any sauce.

alla **CASALINGA:** Homemade, or house-style; will be an herbal sauce, possibly with meat, usually including tomatoes, onions and garlic.

CASONCELLI: Another meat-mixture stuffed pasta, a ravioli.

CHIOCCIOLE: Pasta shaped like a seashell.

CHITARRA: A wire-strung flat frame, like a guitar, on which a sheet of pasta is laid. A rolling pin forces the pasta through the wires, thus cutting them into narrow strips, distance between the wires determining width of noodles so cut.

alla **CIOCIARA:** Roman-country peasant style; served in seasoned meat sauce with fresh butter and grated Parmesan.

alla **CIPOLLA:** Sauce with thinly sliced onions sautéed in oil or lard, and combined with beaten egg. For spaghetti is a sauce of thinly sliced onions gently sautéed in tomato paste mixture.

CONCHIGLIE: Fluted, shell-shaped pasta.

alla **CONTADINA:** Peasant style; a butter sauce of onion, parsley, mushrooms, tomato paste, and served with grated Parmesan.

alle **COZZE:** In a sauce of mussels (in or out of the shell) steamed in olive oil, garlic, parsley, with or without tomatoes.

alla **CREMA:** A white sauce of butter, flour, milk, to which Parmesan cheese and beaten egg yolks have been added.

CRESPOLINI: A flour pancake filled with a mixture of chopped veal and ham, bound with egg and grated cheese; rolled, and baked in tomato sauce.

alla **DIAVOLA:** In a tomato meat sauce with paprika and cayenne pepper.

alla **DUCHESSA:** Duchess style; served in beaten egg yolks, grated Parmesan cheese, melted butter, and topped with sliced chicken livers sautéed in butter.

FARFALLETTE: Butterfly wing-shaped pasta.

PASTA: (cont.)

con **FEGATINI:** In a sauce containing chopped chicken livers.

FETTUCCINE: Actually a noodle. Width varies with region; usually about 3/8". Served with many different sauces. In Rome, two restaurants serve it as a renowned specialty « Fettuccine al Burro ».

FILETTI di POMODORO: Sauce of herbs, olive oil, and peeled, seeded sliced tomatoes.

al **FINANZIERA:** A sauce which may have cock's combs, veal sweetbreads and brains, rabbit livers, but certainly with chicken giblets, herbs, bacon, onion and broth.

alla **FIORENTINA:** In an herbal tomato-meat sauce with green peas.

al **FORNO:** Baked in the oven with a sauce.

ai **FRUTTI di MARE:** A sauce of olive oil, herbs, tomatoes, and pieces of various seafoods.

FUSILLI: Long spiral-shaped solid pasta (twisted).

alla **GENOVESE:** Means al Pesto; a sauce made of a paste of fresh, crushed basil leaves, garlic, olive oil, pine nuts, with added Pecorino cheese.

GHIOTTONA: In a seasoned meat sauce united with a sauce of onion, chicken combs, ovaries, liver, white wine, and mushrooms.

GNOCCHI: A small dumpling made of either semolina flour, flour, cornmeal, rice, or boiled potatoes and flour.

al **Forno:** Baked in the oven with some sort of sauce over them.

alla **Genovese:** Genoa style; potato gnocchi served «al PESTO», in a paste-sauce of olive oil, fresh basil leaves garlic, pine nuts, grated Pecorino cheese.

alla **Napoletana:** Served in an aromatic tomato sauce with chopped basil.

di **Patate:** Made of riced potatoes and flour.

alla **Piemontese:** Made of riced potatoes and flour; served with a tomato herbal sauce and grated Parmesan. In season can also have slices of truffle.

al **Ragu:** Served in an aromatic tomato-meat sauce.

alla **Romana:** Made of semolina flour, eggs, milk, and served baked in the oven with butter and grated Parmesan cheese. They are usually round discs.

alla **Sorrentina:** Usually made of potatoes, and served in casserole with herbal tomato sauce and grated Parmesan.

PASTA: (cont.)

Verde: Green in color. Can be made either of flour with spinach and Ricotta cheese, or of potato with spinach added; served with tomato sauce and grated Parmesan.

GRATINATE: Boiled, then having beaten egg, any of several cheeses mixed through, or a sauce poured over, cheese covered, and browned briefly in oven.

LASAGNE: A wide, flat noodle of varying widths, usually with curly edges, often baked.

al **Burro e Piselli:** Boiled, and served with melted butter, cooked peas, and grated Parmesan.

al **Forno:** This is the most common preparation. Extra wide widths, boiled, and then laid in a casserole with alternating layers of the lasagne, Mozzarella and Ricotta cheese, and a meat-based tomato sauce; then baked in the oven.

con **Funghi:** Boiled, and served with a mushroom sauce.

Pasticciate: Literally, a pie, but basically is the same as « al **Forno** », with wider sheets of lasagne, layered with alternating Mozzarella, meat sauce; then baked in the oven.

al **Pesto:** Boiled, and served in a paste sauce of basil leaves, garlic, pine nuts, grated Pecorino cheese, and olive oil.

Verde: Green lasagne; made by adding spinach to the dough.

Verdi alla Bolognese: Green, baked lasagne, layered with lasagne, creamed white sauce, and Bolognese herbal tomato-meat sauce, and topped with grated Parmesan.

al **LIMONE:** With a sauce of beaten eggs, lemon juice, and grated Parmesan.

LINGUINI: Very narrow flat noodles.

MACCHERONI (CINI): This is our macaroni; a long, or short-cut, medium diameter, hollow tubular pasta. If alla CHITARRA, though, will be a narrow noodle.

alla **Principe di Napoli:** Baked with ham, veal tongue, and cheese.

di **MAGRO:** Sauce with no meat, but with fresh mushrooms, pine nuts, anchovy, tomato, flour, butter and onion; or with tuna, anchovy, parsley, basil, sage and olive oil.

MALLOREDDUS: Tiny dumplings flavored with saffron, and served with meat sauce and grated Pecorino cheese.

PASTA: (cont.)

MALTAGLIATI: Short, diagonally cut tubes (macaroni).

MANICOTTI: A rolled sheet pasta stuffed with Ricotta cheese, meat, herbs, and baked in the oven; served with tomato sauce.

alla **MARINARA:** Sailor's style; a sauce of capers, black olives, garlic, parsley in olive oil.

alla **MATRICIANA:** Same as AMATRICIANA.

NAPOLEONE: After Napoleon; in a sauce of chicken breast, cooked ham, onion, brandy, tomato sauce, broth, butter, and served on sliced cooked eggplant and Mozzarella cheese.

alla **NAPOLETANA:** Naples style: a sauce of lard or olive oil and tomatoes, garlic, onion, topped with grated Parmesan. This is the generally offered non-meat sauce.

NORCINA: A sauce of melted Mozzarella cheese, butter, chopped pork sausage, and green peas.

al **OLIO e AGLIO:** Served with olive oil in which garlic has been simmered, then topped with chopped parsley and grated Parmesan.

ORECCHIETTE: Small, ear-shaped pieces of pasta.

PAGLIA e FIENO: « Straw and hay »; a serving of half of white and half of green noodles, usually with a sauce of butter, fresh mushrooms, garlic, chopped ham, and peas.

con **PAJATA:** A sauce of internal organs of veal, chopped ham, onions, garlic, celery, white wine, and dressed with grated Pecorino cheese.

alla **PANNA:** With cream and grated cheese.

PANZONI (al Sugo di Noce): A ravioli; chopped Swiss Chard and cheese-stuffed squares of sheet pasta served in a sauce of walnuts, basil, garlic, and Parmesan cheese.

PAPPARDELLE: A long, flat, fairly wide (as lasagne) noodle.

al **Sugo di Lepre:** Served with a flour-thickened sauce of bacon, onion, celery, carrot, meat broth, and most important of all, hare meat.

alla **PARTENOPEA:** Poetic name for Naples (alla Napolitana).

PASSATELLI: A fresh pasta of egg, breadcrumbs, Parmesan, passed through a coarse sieve, and cooked in broth.

alla **Romagnola:** Made with beef bone marrow added to the dough.

PASTA: (cont.)

PASTA: The overall, general term for all flour-made products, and when not specified on the menu as to type, it could be any of the noodles, spaghettis, macaronis, etc.

Asciutta: Literally, DRY, but really means served with some type of sauce or dressing. This word is used to distinguish it from PASTA in BRODO (Pasta cooked in, and served in a soup or broth).

e **Ceci:** Boiled, and served mixed with garbanzo beans (chickpeas), in an onion, garlic, tomato sauce.

con **Fagioli:** A paste of cooked dried beans, rosemary, lard, onion, garlic, olive oil, tossed with more cooked beans and hot boiled pasta.

e **Fagioli alla Veneta:** Same as con Fagioli.

e **Fasoi:** Dialect for Fagioli.

alla **Sarda:** See under SARDA.

con **Sarde:** See under SARDE.

PASTICCIO: Literally a pie, but when of pasta is an oven-baked, layered, wide pasta such as lasagne, with cheese, meat sauce, perhaps creamed white sauce.

alla **Ferrarese:** Short, cut macaroni mixed with a mushroom meat sauce, and a creamed white sauce; baked in the oven.

PENNE: Short lengths of tubular, hollow pasta (macaroni), cut diagonally.

al **PESTO:** A Genoa preparation; a paste of fresh, crushed basil leaves, pine nuts, garlic, olive oil, and Pecorino cheese.

alla **PIEMONTESE:** Served with grated Parmesan cheese, white pepper, butter, touch of nutmeg; finished with herbal meat sauce and sliced white truffles.

PINCIGRASSI: A misspelling for VINCIGRASSI (see under the latter).

con **PISELLI:** A sauce of dried meat or sausage, onion, olive oil, garlic, celery, parsley, peas and dill, or just a sauce featuring green peas.

alla **PIZZAIOLA:** A sauce of meat juices, garlic, tomato, olive oil, oregano, and parsley.

POLENTA: A cornmeal mush, solid enough to be cut; can be later baked. It is served with a number of sauces, and as a base or bed on which to place roasted, or braised chicken or game birds; from the north of Italy.

al **POMODORO:** An herbal tomato sauce with onion, garlic, olive oil.

alla **POSILLIPO:** Seafood in herbal tomato sauce.

PASTA: (cont.)

al **PROSCIUTTO:** In an herbal tomato sauce containing chopped cooked ham.

alla **PROVENZALE:** In a sauce of onion, olive oil, tomato, dried mushrooms, and served topped with chopped black olives.

alla **PUTANESCA:** In the style of a lady of ill repute; a tomato sauce with capers, black olives, garlic, and chopped parsley in olive oil.

al **RAGU:** Basically an herbal seasoned tomato-meat sauce with many different ingredients. It is « THE » meat sauce most Americans expect on spaghetti. Bolognese or Sugo mean the same thing.

RAVIOLI: Small, usually square forms of sheet pasta stuffed with various meat, or meat-cheese-vegetable mixtures, boiled, and served with various sauces.

alla **Bolognese:** Either served in an herbal tomato meat sauce, or, likely will be Tortellini, a round doughnut-shaped pasta stuffed with various meats, and served in the Bolognese herbal tomato meat sauce.

alla **Genovese:** This is the ravioli dish as Americans know it; squares of pasta stuffed with a mixture of meat, herbs, spinach; boiled, and served in a meat, tomato, and herb sauce.

alla **Romagnola:** The stuffing is of Ricotta cheese, grated Parmesan, egg and flour (usually no spinach); served in an herbal meat sauce.

alla **RICOTTA ROMANA:** With a tomato sauce with fresh basil and garlic, and then small bits of Ricotta cheese mixed through.

RIGATONI: Large diameter tubular, hollow pasta (macaroni), cut into short lengths.

con la **Pajata:** A sauce of internal organs of veal, chopped ham, onions, garlic, celery, white wine, with the pasta dressed with Pecorino cheese.

ROMAGNOLA: Romagna style (not Rome, but the area including Bologna); a sauce of mashed garlic and parsley, olive oil and tomatoes with grated Parmesan.

alla **ROMANA:** Roman style; served in a seasoned meat sauce with white pepper, butter, grated Parmesan, or can be the same as alla GHIOTTONA.

SALSA di NOCE: Usually served with Panzoni, a ravioli. A sauce of chopped walnuts, basil, garlic, and Parmesan cheese.

alla **SALSA FUNGHI:** In a meat broth mushroom sauce.

PASTA: (cont.)

alla **SARDA:** Sardinian style; in a brown tomato meat sauce with red wine and fresh basil; served with grated Pecorino cheese.

con **SARDE:** A Sicilian preparation subject to many variations. Basically is a sauce of anchovies, fresh sardines, onion, olive oil, a touch of saffron, and if possible, fresh wild fennel, raisins, and pine nuts.

SFORMATO (INO) di BUCATINI: In this case, long, small diameter tubular pasta (macaroni), boiled, then placed in a mold with a meat or cream sauce, and baked in the oven. The Sformato means in a mold.

SPAGHETTI (INI): A long, small diameter solid core round pasta. It lends itself to a multitude of preparations in sauce, and dressings, over 60 of which are listed in this section.

al **SUGO:** Means with sauce; it is normally the RAGU or BOLOGNESE, an herbal tomato meat sauce.

di **Carne:** Same as above; a meat sauce with tomato, herbs, etc.

di **Ciccia:** Another name for meat; the usual meat sauce.

di **Lepre:** An herbal tomato meat sauce, but with meat of the hare.

TAGLIATELLE: A flat noodle which can vary in width from 1/2" to 5/8". There are many different preparations, as with spaghetti. Is frequently house-made, and with egg in the dough.

TAGLIERINI: A fresh, narrow width flat noodle frequently with egg in the dough (all'UOVA).

TAGLIOLINI: A long narrow, flat noodle.

TIMBALE: A crusted casserole dish of some form of pasta (usually a noodle type) layered with mixed chopped meat and/or vegetables, and baked; served with a sauce over it.

TONARRELLI: A very fine string pasta, usually fresh, and made with eggs.

al **TONNO:** A sauce of mashed canned tuna, garlic, tomato, olive oil, capers, and parsley; possibly with a mashed anchovy in it.

TORTELLINI: Small, round, doughnut-shaped, or half-moon stuffed pasta.

alla **Bolognese:** Stuffed with ham, beef marrow, baloney, grated Parmesan, and served in an herbal, tomato meat sauce.

PASTA: (cont.)

TORTELLONE: A large-sized, half-moon shaped stuffed pasta, considered coarser than the smaller Tortellini.

TRENETTE: A medium to narrow width flat noodle; the Genoa name for it.

al **Pesto:** This is the Genoa style; boiled, and served in the al Pesto sauce.

TUBETTI: Short cut tubular pasta (macaroni); salad-size macaroni.

all'**UOVO:** Meaning made with egg in the dough.

VERDE: Green; in pasta it means having had spinach worked into the dough.

VERMICELLI: Small to very small diameter spaghetti.

VINCESGLASS or VINCIGRASSI: A sort of lasagne al forno, but with a more pastry-like pasta, made with alternating layers of creamed white sauce, and chicken liver, mushroom meat sauce, and baked in the oven.

alle **VONGOLE:** In a sauce of clams, olive oil, butter, garlic, chopped parsley, with or without tomato in it.

UOVA
(Egg Dishes)

In Italy, eggs are not served for breakfast as they are in many other countries. The menus which have a separate listing for egg dishes offer them mainly as a first course, or a light main course.

While all traditional methods of cooking eggs are employed, such as AFFOGATE (poached), in TEGAMINO, FRITTE, or al PIATTO (different ways of frying eggs), STRAPAZZATE (scrambled), al FORNO (baked), BOLLITE (boiled), in COCOTTE (shirred), the most popular preparation is some type of omelette.

An OMELETTE, the classic French one, which goes by the same name in Italy, is made of beaten eggs combined with all types of ingredients as FORMAGGIO (cheese), PROSCIUTTO (ham), FUNGHI (mushrooms), FEGATINI di POLLO (chicken livers), ERBE (fresh herbs), FRUTTI di MARE (seafood), which act as a filling, or are mixed in with the beaten eggs. Omelettes are served folded, rolled or flat.

A FRITTATA consists of beaten eggs combined with cooked, diced vegetables, cheese, ham, herbs, or any combination of these, served as a flat omelette.

A TORTINO is made of cooked vegetables, often combined with cheese or ham, added to a beaten egg and milk mixture, and poured into a pie pan which can be lined with a pastry shell or slices of bread, and baked in the oven, to make a kind of egg pie.

UOVA
(Egg Dishes)

AFFOGATE: Poached eggs.

AMERICANA (all'): Fried eggs served with slices of grilled bacon and a half a grilled tomato.

ASPARAGI (con): With asparagus tips.

BACON (al): With bacon.

BARROTTE: Very soft-boiled eggs.

BOLLITE: Soft-boiled eggs.

BURRO (al): Fried in butter.

CAMICIA (in): Poached eggs.

CAMPAGNOLA (alla): With diced cooked vegetables, herbs, cheese.

CAPRICCIOSA (alla): Poached eggs, served in a hollowed-out piece of fried bread with a Marsala wine-flavored sauce and bacon.

CARCIOFI (di) (con): With artichoke hearts.

CARDINALE (al): With seafood, mushrooms, truffles - - an omelette filling.

CASALINGA (alla): Implying home-style cooking.

COCOTTE (in): Shirred eggs. The eggs are placed in small, individual earthenware or porcelain casseroles, poached in a pan of simmering water in the oven, or on top of the stove.

CONFETTURA (alla): With jam, a filling for a sweet omelette.

COQUE (alla): Soft-boiled eggs.

ERBE (alle): With finely chopped fresh herbs.

FARCITE: Stuffed hard-boiled eggs.

FEGATINI di POLLO (con): With sautéed chicken livers.

FIORENTINA (alla): Poached eggs served with spinach and grated Parmesan cheese, or a spinach filling for an omelette served with a cheese sauce.

FONDUTA: A hot melted cheese mixture containing chunks of Fontina or Groviera (Swiss) cheese, milk, cornstarch, egg yolks, and topped with sliced white truffles. Toasted bread is dipped into the mixture, or it is served over rice or polenta, a thick cornmeal mush.

FORMAGGIO (al) (con): With cheese.

FORNO (al): Baked eggs.

FRITTATA: Beaten eggs combined with various cooked, diced vegetables, cheese, ham, herbs, or combinations of these, and served as a flat omelette. The ingredient which gives it its particular name you can identify in this section in its alphabetical order. For example, to translate FRITTATA con SPINACI, look under SPINACI (spinach).

FRITTE: Eggs fried in abundant butter or oil - - basted.

FRUTTI di MARE: With seafood.

FUNGHI (con): With mushrooms.

GELATINA (in): In aspic.

GROVIERA (al): With Gruyere or Swiss cheese.

GUSCIO (al): Soft-boiled eggs.

LARDO (con): With bacon.

MARMELLATA (con): With jam filling, or sweet omelette.

MOLLETTE: Medium-boiled eggs.

MOZZARELLA in CARROZZA: « Cheese in a Carriage » - - small squares or rounds of sliced white bread with slices of soft, mild, white Mozzarella cheese between them, dipped in an egg batter and deep-fried.

OCCHIO di BUE (all'): Another expression for fried eggs, the same as al Piatto.

OMELETTE: The classic French type is made of beaten eggs combined with all types of ingredients as cheese, ham, fresh herbs, seafood, chicken livers, pureed vegetables, which act as a filling, or are mixed in with the eggs. Omelettes are served folded, rolled or flat. The ingredient which gives it its particular name you can identify in this section in its alphabetical order. For example, to translate OMELETTE al FORMAGGIO, look under FORMAGGIO (cheese).

PAESANA (alla): Peasant style - - with vegetables and diced bacon or ham.

PANCETTA AFFUMICATA: Smoked bacon.

PARMIGIANA (alla): With Parmesan cheese.

PIATTO (al): Fried eggs. Done in a frying pan in butter or oil.

POMODORO (al) (con): With tomatoes.

PORTOGHESE: With tomato paste and tomato sauce.

PROSCIUTTO (con) (al): With ham.

RIPIENE: Stuffed hard-boiled eggs.

SEMPLICE: Plain, as a plain omelette.

SODE: Hard-boiled eggs.

con **Maionese:** Served with mayonnaise.

SPAGNOLA (alla): With tomatoes, bell peppers and garlic or onions.

SPINACI (con): With spinach.

STRACCIATE: Scrambled eggs.

STRAPAZZATE: Scrambled eggs.

TEGAME, TEGAMINO (al) (in): Fried eggs cooked in oil or butter in a small, individual frying pan with two loop handles, in which they are served.

TORTINO: Cooked vegetables, often combined with cheese or ham, or both, added to a beaten egg and milk mixture and poured into a pie pan lined with pastry shell or slices of bread, and baked in the oven, to make a kind of egg pie. The famous TORTINO DI CARCIOFI alla TOSCANA is made without a crust, so it is more of a FRITTATA (flat omelette). The ingredient which gives the TORTINO its particular name you can identify in this section in its alphabetical order. For example, to translate TORTINO di ZUCCHINI look under ZUCCHINI (Italian squash).

TURKA (alla): Shirred eggs, baked in individual dish with sautéed chicken livers.

VERDURA (con): With vegetables.

ZUCCHINI (con) (di): With zucchini or Italian squash.

PESCE e FRUTTI DI MARE
(Fish and Seafood)

Because Italy is surrounded by the sea, except in the North, and where, in that region there are large lakes and rivers, fish make up an important part of the diet, and the fish section of the menu offers a wide and varying array of fish and seafood dishes throughout the country.

Many of the provinces and areas have their own names for these creatures, so you may encounter several different names for the same item. These cities or areas also have their separate preparations for the fish, but frequently the cooking or preparation varies only slightly.

Where a dish or preparation is renowned, or when it is one which will be constantly encoutered on menus, it has been described rather completely. Many of the fish do not exist in the United States, and so the name in English, where possible, has been further described by its resemblance to some American fish with which you are familiar,

PESCE e FRUTTI DI MARE
(Fish and Seafood)

Two standard cooking methods, when they do not involve any special preparation, appear for so many fish that we list them here rather than repeat them over and over.

1. ai **FERRI:** Literally « on iron » - - grilled on a flat or ridged steel plate after being marinated in an herbal olive oil and brushed with the same during grilling.

2. alla **GRIGLIA:** Grilled, same as « ai Ferri ».

ACCIUGHE: Anchovies, usually canned.

ACQUADELLA: Small 3''-4'' Whitebait-like fish used for FRITTO (deep-frying).

ALICI: Anchovies, either filets salt-cured and canned in olive oil, or fresh.

in **Tortiera:** Fresh anchovies, breaded and fried in olive oil.

ANGUILLA: Eel.

Carpionata: Floured and fried, served cold in herbal vinegar marinade.

alla **Fiorentina:** Florence style - - cut into pieces, floured, browned in olive oil, then baked in oven with garlic, sage leaves, the oil, and red wine.

48

ANGUILLA: (cont.)

in **Umido:** Braised - - browned in oil, onion and parsley, then simmered in added tomato paste and water.

alla **Veneziana:** Cooked in a sauce containing tuna and lemon juice.

ARAGOSTA: Spiny lobster (actually a sea crayfish), the California type, no claws.

all'**Americana:** Tail pieces cooked in a tomato-base sauce of onion, carrot, shallots, parsley, bay leaf, white wine, and possibly garlic, chervil, thyme and cream. There are a number of variations of this dish, but always with tomato.

Bollita: Boiled, usually served cold with mayonnaise.

alla **Griglia:** Grilled, but usually on a flat steel plate, not over charcoal.

ARSELLE: Mussels, the clam-like looking sea mollusc with dark blue shell and orange meat.

ASTACO: True lobster with claws, the Maine lobster, not found in the Mediterranean.

ASTICI: Can be name for Astaco, or also for SCAMPI (prawns).

BACCALA: Dried, salt-cured Codfish, soaked in water to de-salt and soften it for cooking.

Fritto: Fried, usually deep-fried, and can be floured first.

alla **Livornese:** Braised in sauce of olive oil, white wine, tomatoes, carrots, celery, onions, with cooked tripe slices.

con **Polenta:** Braised in a sauce of olive oil base, and served either with, or on a bed of polenta, a thick cornmeal mush mixture.

al **Pomodoro:** Braised in herbal tomato sauce.

alla **Vicentina:** Floured, braised in a sauce of wine, oil, milk, herbs, anchovies, parsley, onion and garlic.

BIANCHETTI: Tiny, pure white anchovy or sardine fry, barely hatched from the egg. They are either fried or boiled, and served cold with oil and lemon juice.

BRANZINO: A Sea bass, or in some areas can be a Sea perch.

Bollito: Simmered in water and white wine containing herbs, onions, carrot.

alla **Fiamma:** Braised in a sauce of some kind, and then flamed with brandy.

BRANZINOTTI: Small Branzinos, or a Bream-shaped (vertically flattish) sea fish.

BURRIDA: A fish casserole, usually with seafood added; cooked with onion, garlic, carrots, celery, chopped parsley, anchovies, tomatoes, dried mushrooms in olive oil. A cross between a soup and a stew, similar to a Bouillabaisse. A meal in itself.

CALAMAI: Squid.

con **Erbe:** Squid, cut up and simmered in herbal olive oil sauce.

CALAMARETTI: Small baby squid.

Fritti: Marinated in herbal olive oil, floured, then deep-fried.

alla **Luciana:** Braised, or stewed in a sealed pot in oil sauce of red bell peppers, tomatoes, parsley, fresh basil.

allo **Spiedino:** Baby squid marinated in herbal olive oil, skewered, and cooked either over charcoal, or on a flat steel grill plate.

CALAMARI: Squid.

alla **Brace:** Broiled over live coals after having been marinated in herbal olive oil.

Cassuola di: Sliced squid braised in herbal olive oil, usually also with tomatoes.

Fritto di: Sliced squid breaded or floured, and deep-fried.

CALAMITO: Another name for Grey Mullet.

CANNOCCHIE: An odd sea creature, a prawn-shrimp like crustacean which looks about the same at each end. Has a number of names.

CAPITONE: A variety of eel.

al **Forno:** Pieces marinated in oil, wine, and herbs, and baked in this marinade.

CAPPON MAGRO: A Genoa specialty - - it is a combination vegetable and seafood salad. Layers of diced, cooked vegetables and boiled seafood, formed into a mound and served with a mayonnaise-type sauce flavored with garlic, pinenuts, herbs and capers.

CARPA: Carp, a fresh water fish.

CARPIONE: Carp, or rarely, also a lake-trout type fish.

alla **Fiamma:** Marinated in herbal olive oil, brushed with bread crumbs, and grilled over live coals.

CEFALO: Grey Mullet.

CERNIA: A sea fish with large head (1/3 of its body); varies in size.

Trancia di: Slice of Cernia.

Arrosto: Slice marinated in herbal olive oil, floured, then baked in this marinade.

CERNIA: (cont.)

    Livornese: Slice braised in tomato sauce of olive oil, garlic, parsley and celery.

CICALE di MARE: Literally, a sea grass-hopper, another name for Cannocchie.

CODA di ROSPO: Tail of the Rospo, or Angler fish, or Frog fish. The Rospo has a huge head tapering down to the tail, which length, after the head, is the part eaten. It has a flaky flesh.

COZZE: One of the many names for mussels - - the clam-like mollusc with the dark blue-black shell and orange meat. (See also MOSCOLI or MUSCOLI).

    alla **Livornese:** Mussels braised in their shells in aromatic tomato sauce, served on a slice of toasted or fried bread.

    alla **Marinara:** Steamed in oil, white wine, garlic. (See also MOSCOLI or MUSCOLI).

    Pepata di, or **Impepata di,** or **Impazzata di:** Mussels served in a sauce of oil, garlic, parsley, and black pepper.

DATTERI di MARE: A sea date literally, which is a mussel with shell shaped like a date, or a small razor clam.

DENTICE: A vertically flat Mediterranean fish, similar in shape to a Pompano or Bream, slightly hump-backed with prominent teeth. Called in England a Toothed Gilthead.

    Bollito: Simmered gently in water with onion, carrot, parsley, thyme, bay leaf, vinegar, salt and whole peppercorns.

FERRI (ai): Literally « on iron » - - grilled on a flat or ridged steel plate.

FILETTO (I) di PESCE: Filets of some kind of fish.

    alla **Milanese:** Breaded (floured, dipped in beaten egg, then in bread crumbs) and pan-fried to a golden color.

FRITTO (I): Fried, or usually deep-fried items.

    di **Calamaretti e Gamberi:** Floured and deep-fried sliced baby squid and prawns.

    Misto del Golfo: Deep-fried mixture of floured small-cut squid, prawns, etc.

    Misto Mare: Floured and deep-fried mixed seafoods and little fish.

    Misto del Paese: Various local fish and seafoods deep-fried.

    Misto Scampi: Deep-fried prawns.

FRITTURA del PAESE: Same as Fritto Misto del Paese.

FRUTTI di MARE: A plate of various seafoods - - squid, mussels, either raw, steamed or fried.

GAMBERELLI: Shrimps.

GAMBERETTI: Very small shrimps, but someone may apply this name to a larger pink one.

GAMBERO (I): Here confusion enters. Basically this is a large shrimp or medium prawn, but also this same name is applied to fresh-water crayfish or crawdads, the ones with pincers, and also to the langoustine, a salt-water crayfish also with pincers, but smaller than the Maine lobster. The true lobster, the Maine type, does not occur in the Mediterranean, but if imported, might also be called a GAMBERO or ASTACO. Then, a GAMBERO in one area is a GAMBERONI in another. Best to say that it is a medium-sized prawn.

    Bollito: Boiled, served cold with mayonnaise or tartar sauce.

    alla **Salsa Tartara:** Boiled and served cold with tartar sauce.

GAMBERONI: Large-sized prawns.

GANOCCHIO: Another name for the CANNOCCHIE the fore-aft sort of prawn.

GRANCEOLA (EVOLA): An Adriatic sea crab.

    alla **Veneziana:** Crab which is boiled, seasoned with oil, lemon juice, pepper, and served in its own shell.

GRANCHIO: Also a crab, or can be just the crabmeat.

GRIGLIA (alla): Grilled, same as « ai Ferri ».

INSALATA di PESCE: Fish salad, a seafood salad containing boiled squid, mussels, clams. Usually served with an oil and lemon juice dressing, but can also be heavily mayonnaised.

LAMPREDA: Lamprey, a type of sea eel.

LINGUA: A name for Sole, the horizontally flat sea fish.

LUPO di MARE: A Sea bass, literally, a sea wolf.

MACCARELLO: Mackerel.

MAZZANCOLLE: A large prawn, could also be called a Gambero or Gamberoni.

MERLANO: A Whiting, a sea fish similar to the Hake or Codfish.

MERLUZZO (I): Codfish. **MERLUZZETTI:** Small Codfish.

    Fritto: Floured, dipped in beaten egg, then breaded and fried.

    al **Gratin:** Filets of Codfish breaded, and baked in the oven with a mixture of mashed anchovy and chopped parsley spread over.

MISTO (I): Means mixed, but is short for mixed fried sea-food and fish dishes.

MITILO: Another name for the mussel.

MOLLETTE: Medium-boiled eggs.

MORMORA (E): A small vertically flat sea fish with firm flesh.

al **Forno:** Baked in an aromatic herbal oil sauce, basted with white wine.

MOSCARDINO (I): Small squid.

alla **Genovese:** Braised in sauce of onion, olive oil, parsley, garlic, tomato paste, dry mushrooms, rosemary, and served on a slice of crisp fried bread.

alla **Luciana:** Braised in a sauce of olive oil, basil, rosemary, mushrooms, tomato sauce.

MOSCOLI (MOSCIOLI): Mussels; the orange-fleshed mollusc with a dark blue-black shell.

MUSCOLI: Mussels, same as above. (See also COZZE).

al **Agro:** Agro implies sour, acidy or tart; hence, served with lemon juice.

Arrosto: Mussels in half-shell covered with a filling of bread crumbs, herbs, chopped ham, grated cheese, tomato sauce, and then baked.

al **Gratin (Gratinati):** Braised in olive oil, herbs, white wine; then served on the half-shell after being sprinkled with bread crumbs and put under broiler. Or, less commonly, cooked in shell in oil, and served on half-shell with a thick, white wine cream sauce.

alla **Marinara:** Mussels steamed (as with steamed clams), and when opened, served in a soup plate with their juices, oil, chopped garlic, and parsley. Or, may be steamed in these ingredients, and so served; or more rarely, steamed, then removed from shells, and gently simmered in white wine, vinegar, with garlic and parsley previously browned in olive oil with mashed filets of anchovy and fresh basil.

NASELLO: A name for the Whiting or Silver Hake, a Codfish-like fish.

in **Bianco:** Poached in white wine and water with herbs. Served hot.

Bollito: Simmered in aromatic fish stock of herbs, onion, olive oil, etc.

OCCHIATE: The Orata, or Pompano-shaped Sea Bream (vertically flat).

OMBRINA: A smallish Sea bass or Sea perch.

OMBRINA: (cont.)

Trancia di, in Gratella: Grilled slice of Sea bass, marinated, and brushed during grilling with the marinade oil. Gratella is same as alla Griglia - - grilled.

ORATA: Mediterranean fish, vertically flat and similar in shape to the Pompano or Bream.

al **Cartoccio:** Small Sea Bream covered with moistened chopped dry mushrooms, chopped parsley, mussels, and shrimp, and baked enclosed in an envelope of buttered paper or foil.

ORATINO: A small Orata.

OSTRICHE: Oysters, not much found in Italy, except in the South, especially Taranto on the Adriatic.

PAGARO (PAGRO): A sea fish similar in shape to the Dentice or Gilthead, Pompano in shape.

al **Forno:** Baked in herbal oil, with or without tomatoes.

PALOMBO: The Dogfish, a Barricuda-diametered, long, relatively narrow grey-skinned fish.

Bollito: Poached in water with white wine, herbs, carrot, onion, and served either hot with melted butter, or cold with appropriate sauce.

Braciole di: A chop or cutlet of, i.e., a slice, could be grilled or baked.

alla **Milanese:** Slices in egg, breaded, and deep-fried.

PANNOCCHIE: Livorno name for PANNOCCHIE.

PEOCI: Venice area name for mussels (See MOSCOLI).

PESCATRICE: The Angler fish or Rospo (See Coda di Rospo, or Rospo).

PESCE: Could be any fish - - merely FISH.

Arrosto: Marinated in oil with herbs, such as sage, basil, rosemary, parsley, with or without mashed garlic, bay leaf, thyme, usually floured, and then baked in this marinade.

in **Bianco:** Simmered or poached in white wine, water, vinegar, herbs, carrot, celery, onion, and served either hot or cold, usually with an appropriate sauce.

Carpionata, or in Carpione: Marinated in herbal oil, floured, fried, and then further marinated in herbal vinegar and served cold.

al **Cartoccio:** Marinated in herbal oil, covered with an herbal paste of anchovies, or seafoods, and baked in sealed envelope of oiled or buttered paper or foil.

al **Forno:** Fish baked in oil with or without tomato, and with garlic, sage, bay leaf, lemon juice, and basted with white wine, or variations of these ingredients.

PESCE: (cont.)

Lesso, Lessato: Same as in Bianco, boiled, but actually simmered in herbal broth, wine.

Misto Griglia: Same as grilled, but implies various little fishes, or pieces of fish.

in **Umido:** Pieces of fish braised, uncovered in an herbal sauce and tomato paste, onion, carrot, garlic, oil, water. Actually sort of gently stewed.

PESCE PERSICO: Fresh water Perch. Usually from the Italian lakes.

alla **Milanese:** Filets of Perch, floured, egg-dipped, breaded, and fried in butter, served with chopped parsley and a slice of lemon.

PESCE SAN PIETRO: The John Dory, similar to the Porgy or Scup, a vertically flat fish.

Filetto di, alla Mugnaia: Filets of the St. Peter fish, rolled in flour and fried in butter, topped with chopped parsley and a slice of lemon.

PESCE SPADA: Swordfish.

PIACERE (A): Of your choice, or as you like it prepared.

PIDOCCHI: Again, a name for mussels.

POLIPO (I): Small squid, or very small octopus-like sea creatures, or just Octopus.

Affogato: Poached or simmered in water, white wine, with herbs, and with or without tomatoes or tomato paste.

alla **Luciana:** Braised in oil, garlic, parsley, piquant red peppers (but not a hot dish, very little pepper), tomato and white wine.

in **Umido:** A sort of stew of very small octopi done in olive oil, white or red wine, garlic, anchovies mashed, tomato sauce, parsley, and possibly with dried mushrooms.

POLPO (I): Octopus, same as POLIPO - - they interchange the names.

RAGNO: Same fish as BRANZINO and SPIGOLA, a Sea bass; or Sea perch in some areas.

Bollito: Boiled, but actually simmered gently or poached in water, white wine, some vinegar, herbs, onion, carrot.

RANE: Frogs, or Frog legs.

RANOCCHI: Frogs.

RICCI: Sea urchins, the little spiny ball creature, usually eaten raw.

RIGHINI: Small Bluegill-like fish about 6 inches long.

ROMBO: The name for the Brill, as well as for the Turbot, a Flounder-like sea fish.

ROSPO, CODA di: The Angler fish, a large head tapering down to the tail. The length of fish from head back is the part eaten, and is called the tail.

>**Bollita:** Simmered or poached in herbal water and white wine with onion, carrot, celery, served hot; or cold with mayonnaise, or melted or browned butter.

SALMONE: Salmon, imported, either fresh or smoked.

SAN PIETRO (PESCE SAN PIETRO): Called in England the John Dory, similar to our Porgy or Scup, a vertically swimming flat fish.

>**Filetto di, alla Mugnaia:** Filets of this fish rolled in flour, and fried golden in butter, topped with chopped parsley and a slice of lemon.

SARAGO (SARAGHI): Small vertically swimming flat fish like Bluegill, from the sea.

SARDE: Sardines.

SARDINE: Sardines.

SARDONCINI: Little sardines.

SCAMPI: Actually a large prawn, best of which comes from the Adriatic, but, again, there is confusion, for a salt water crayfish can be called a Scampi, and what is a Gambero in one place will be called a Scampi in another.

>all'**Americana:** Prawns simmered in a tomato sauce of onion, carrot, white wine, shallots, parsley, bay leaf, and possibly cream and a touch of cayenne pepper.

>**Arrosto:** Marinated in herbal oil, and baked in the marinade - - may also have tomato paste added and water, or tomatoes.

>**Dorati:** Floured, or egg-dipped and breaded, and deep-fried golden.

>**Fritti di:** Floured and deep-fried.

>**Spiedino di:** Grilled or broiled on a skewer.

>alla **Veneziana:** Venice style - - boiled, served cold with lemon juice.

SEPPIA (IOLINE): A small Cuttlefish sea creature, looking halfway between a squid and a tiny octopus.

>alla **Livornese:** Small Cuttlefish simmered in sauce of olive oil, onion, parsley, garlic, water, tomato paste, and when in season, with strings of narrow strips of spinach, filets of anchovy, olives, and herbs, and braised in an herbal fish broth.

SEPPIA (IOLINE): (cont.)

 alla **Veneta:** Marinated in oil with garlic, then simmered in this marinade with added white wine. The ink of the fish may or may not be added to the sauce, and if it is the sauce will be a dark purplish-black color.

 alla **Veneziana:** Simmered in sauce or oil, white wine, garlic, broth, parsley and tomato paste.

SGOMBRO (I): Mackerel.

 con **Salsa:** Grilled, boiled, or baked, and served with an appropriate sauce. This is vague, but appears frequently on menus.

SOGLIOLA (E): Sole, the horizontally swimming flat sea fish, so prized.

 all'**Arlecchino:** Poached in fish stock, and served in a fish-based cream sauce containing tomatoes, onions, garlic, butter, and slices of zucchini squash.

 Arrosto: Sole, whole, baked in herbal olive oil and basted with white wine.

 Bollita: Poached in fish stock, and served with suitable sauce, usually a rich creamed one.

 Dorata: Dipped in flour, beaten egg (perhaps then bread crumbs) and fried golden.

 Fritta: Usually filets dipped in flour and deep-fried.

 al **Gratin:** Can be done several ways, from being baked in oven till sauce is browned (a cream sauce with sliced mushrooms, parsley, chopped shallots), to a strictly Italian way of marinating it in base of olive oil, chopped garlic, lemon juice, oregano, then breaded, and broiled as it is basted with the marinade.

 Margherita: Poached in white wine and herbs, and served covered with a Hollandaise sauce.

 alla **Mugnaia:** A la Meunière, or Miller's wife's style - - rolled in flour, and fried golden in butter and oil, and served topped with chopped parsley and a slice of lemon.

 alla **Partenopea:** (Naples style) - - Poached in fish stock or white wine or both, served on bed of macaroni, and covered with cheese and creamed white sauce.

 a **Piacere:** To please you, or to your choice of cooking. State how you want it prepared. There are probably another 161 different, recognized ways of cooking Sole, some elaborate and involved. It is hoped that the above will familiarize you with a few of the most commonly offered preparations.

PESCE

SPARNOCCHIE: Final name for cannocchie, that prawn-shrimp-like crustacean. This is the large-sized one.

SPIEDINO MARE: Mixed pieces of fish and seafoods marinated, and then skewered, and broiled or grilled.

SPIGOLA (E): Sea bass, similar to U.S. Groupers.

> **Arrosto:** Baked Sea bass - - marinated in herbal oil, floured, and baked in the marinade.

STOCCAFISSO: Another name for salt-dried member of the Codfish family. It is soaked in water to de-salt it and soften it before it is cooked.

> all'**Anconetana:** Simmered in a tomato sauce of celery, garlic, rosemary, capers, olive oil and butter.

STORIONE: Sturgeon, the fish that gives the true caviar.

> **Affumicato:** Smoked Sturgeon.

> alla **Milanese:** Slice of Sturgeon breaded and fried golden in butter and oil.

TARTUFI di MARE: Sea truffles - - a small clam with concentric grooves on its shell.

TINCA (CHE): Tench in England - - a fresh water coarse fish with a yellowish skin. It is similar to Bass or Goldfish.

> in **Carpione:** Tench fried in olive oil, and then marinated in herbal vinegar, and served cold.

> **Ripiene al Forno:** Stuffed with mushrooms, egg, herbs, mashed anchovies, bread crumbs, and then baked in the oven.

TONNO: Tuna fish. Served frequently, canned in olive oil, as well as fresh-cooked.

TOTANI: Small Cuttlefish, also called Calamaretti on the Adriatic coast.

> **Fritti:** Fried - - normally floured and deep-fried in conjunction with shrimps.

TRANCIA: Means a slice, could be of any fish.

> alla **Livornese:** Braised in olive oil, garlic, celery, parsley and tomato.

> alla **Napoletana:** Naples style - - braised in olive oil, peppers, parsley, oregano, fresh tomatoes, with or without garlic.

> di **Pesce Bollito:** Slice of poached fish, done in white wine and water with herbs.

> di **Pesce Spada:** Slice of Swordfish.

TRIGLIE: Red Mullet, a Mediterranean delicacy, does not grow very large (10" or so).

> **Arrosto:** Baked, usually in aromatic herbal olive oil and white wine.

TRIGLIE: (cont.)

 al **Cartoccio:** Oiled, covered with paste of mashed onion, dried mushrooms, cooked ham (or Fontina cheese), parsley, and encased in a sealed envelope of buttered paper or foil, and baked in the oven.

 Fritte: Floured and then pan or deep-fried.

 alla **Livornese:** Braised in sauce of olive oil, tomatoes, celery, parsley and garlic, possibly with some thyme in the oil.

TROTA: Trout. Usually they are privately reared. Many are rainbows, originally from the U.S.

 Arrosto: Marinated in herbal oil, baked in this marinade and basted with white wine.

 Bleue: The French « Au Bleu » - - boiled, and served with melted butter or cold with mayonnaise.

 Bollita: Poached in white wine with water and herbs.

 al **Burro:** Fried in butter, may be floured first.

 alla **Maionese:** Poached as in Bollita, and served either covered with an aromatic mayonnaise, or with mayonnaise as a side dressing.

 alla **Mandorla:** Stuffed with slices of onion, parsley; seasoned, buttered, and baked in cream with slices of almonds lying along the length.

 Salmonate: Trout with salmon-colored flesh.

 Salsa Mandorle: Baked in herbal butter, and served in an almond cream sauce with sliced almonds as a garnish.

 Spaccata al Burro: Scored diagonally across the sides, and fried in butter.

TROTELLA: Name normally used to designate lake Trout, which are usually larger than the reared or stream Trout.

VENTRESCA di TONNO: The belly part of the Tuna fish, claimed to be the best part of the fish. This is usually canned in olive oil.

VONGOLE: Clams.

This is by no means the complete list of all Italian fishes, but is one which will cover most fish and seafoods found on Italian menus. In the preparations, you will encounter variations according to the chef's inspiration or preferences.

PIATTI del GIORNO o da FARSI
(Meat, or Main Dishes)

In order to organize this section for rapidity of translation, or untangling, a burden has been placed on you. It will be necessary to learn to recognize the five or six names involved concerning the animals: VITELLO (veal); BUE (beef); MANZO (steer); MAIALE (pork); ABBACCHIO or AGNELLO (lamb); POLLO (chicken).

Thus, when you see, for instance, GIRELLO di VITELLO al MADERA you will find GIRELLO listed alphabetically as a sub-heading under VITELLO. But, certain words and expressions are so well-known to Italians that the type of animal from which they come is not given on the menu. GIRELLO is such a word. We have listed these words again, separately, in their proper alphabetical place, along with their various preparations. For another example, SCALOPPINE di VITELLO will be offered simply as SCALOPPINE.

If you do not find a main dish in this section, then it must be either fish (listed under PESCE section), or wild game (listed under CACCIAGIONE section, which begins at the end of this PIATTI del GIORNO section).

ai **FERRI** and alla **GRIGLIA**, both meaning **GRILLED,** and alla **BRACE** meaning charcoal broiled apply to many different meats. They are not usually repeated under the individual meat involved.

FOR YOUR STEAKS: RARE is al **SANGUE; MEDIUM RARE** is al **PUNTO: WELL DONE** is **BEN COTTO.**

(See BREAKDOWN OF THE MENU (pg. 15) for other expressions meaning MAIN DISHES).

PIATTI del GIORNO o da FARSI
(Meat, or Main Dishes)

ABBACCHIO: Milk-fed lamb.

Braciole d', a Scottadito: Tiny grilled lamb chops.

Braciolette d': Grilled lamb chops or cutlets.

Brodettato: Small pieces of lamb sautéed in a white wine sauce thickened with beaten egg yolks; flavored with lemon juice.

alla **Cacciatora:** Pieces of lamb braised in lard with rosemary, garlic, sage, vinegar and water. Before serving, mashed anchovies are added to the gravy.

ABBACCHIO: (cont.)

> **Costolette d', alla Griglia:** Grilled or broiled lamb chops.

al **Forno:** Roasted - - a specialty in Rome.

allo **Spiedo:** Roasted on a spit.

AGNELLO: Lamb.

> **Arrosto:** Roast lamb, usually leg.

> **Bistecca d':** Loinsteak of lamb, or could be from the leg.

> **Corata d', alla Salvia:** Internal organs of lamb: heart, liver, kidneys; broiled, fried, or braised with sage leaves flavoring the cooking.

> **Costole alla Milanese:** Milan style; breaded lamb chops fried golden, in butter.

al **Forno:** Roast lamb, usually leg.

> **Tracciole d':** Skewered lamb pieces interspersed with vegetables - - a shishkebab of sorts.

alla **Turca:** A Lamb stew with raisins added to the gravy.

AMBURGHESE alla TIROLESE: Hamburger patty served with fried, or French-fried onion rings.

AMBURGO, BURRO e SALVIA: Hamburger patty fried in butter and topped with sage leaf.

ANIMELLE: Sweetbreads.

alla **Marsala:** Sweetbreads cooked in a Marsala wine sauce.

> **Tegamino d':** Merely means served in a little two-handled frying pan, but are usually floured, fried in butter, and served covered with grated hard-boiled egg.

ARISTA: Loin of pork, usually with bone in.

alla **Fiorentina:** The well-known Tuscany preparation. Rubbed with, or having stuck into it a paste of garlic, rosemary, cloves, salt and pepper, and roasted in the oven, or turned on a spit.

al **Forno:** Roast loin of pork.

di **Suino:** Another expression for pork loin.

ARROSTI MISTI FREDDI: Slices of cold roasted meats.

ARROSTINO ANNEGATO con FUNGHI: Small roast (usually veal) served, as they say, « drowned » in mushrooms.

ARROSTO: A roast; roasted.

alla **Genovese:** Veal or beef pot-roast in gravy of onion, carrot, tomato paste, dried mushrooms, broth, white wine.

alla **Montanara:** Veal or beef roast with browning brew of garlic, onion, olive oil, rosemary, twigs of juniper, broth. It is more of a pot-roast.

ARROSTO: (cont.)

    Morto al Forno: Morto means pot-roasted; i.e., little liquid, and cooked covered, slowly, for a long time.

con **Pastine:** A roast with a crust, usually of dough.

BAGARD: An obscure word for PAILLARD of veal; a chop, or more precisely, a cutlet.

BAGNA CAUDA: Raw vegetables such as celery, bell peppers, cauliflower, fennel, dipped into a pot of boiling olive oil, butter, garlic and chopped anchovies. Cream, Barbera red wine and/or white truffles may be added. A Piedmont specialty and a winter dish, eaten with bread and cheese.

BATTUTA SCANELLO: Literally, beaten or pounded slice of round steak of veal, or beef, but could also mean ground or minced. Depends on the chef.

BATTUTINA al PROSCIUTTO: Hamburger mixed with raw, cured ham.

BISTECCA: Meaning beefsteak, but can be a boneless cut of practically any meat, and is usually from leg or sirloin area; can even be from chicken.

    Arrosto: Roast loin of beef; could be from prime rib area on back to porterhouse, but without filet.

alla **Bismark:** Loin (T-bone, without bone), butter-fried steak served topped with a fried egg.

alla **Fiorentina:** This is THE steak of Italy. Origin: Florence in Tuscany. It is usually a rib steak with bone in, but can be a T-bone, or even a porterhouse. Is considered huge, but is actually only about 10 oz. for a single, or a little over a pound for two, and comes from baby beef, or fairly matured steer. It is broiled over charcoal after it has been salted and peppered and coated with olive oil. Served with lemon wedge.

    di **Manzo ai Ferri:** Grilled beefsteak.

alla **Pizzaiola:** Boneless T-bone steak fried or grilled, and served covered with a sauce of garlic, tomatoes, parsley, and oregano in olive oil.

    al **Tartufo:** Grilled steak served topped with sliced or grated truffles.

BOCCONCINI: Literally means a mouthful, implying a certain lusciousness or mouthwatering appeal. Thus it can be whatever the chef dreams up, and can bear whatever name he gives it.

    Cacciatora: Small pieces of steak sauteed in oil and butter with mushrooms and herbs,

BOCCONCINI: (cont.)

alla **Casalinga:** Meaning home-style; small pieces of meat sauteed in oil and herbs.

alla **Fiorentina:** Sauteed pieces of steak in herbs, garlic, and onion.

di **Vitello con Piselli:** Small pieces of veal sauteed in herbal sauce and served with peas.

BOLLITO: Meaning boiled; generally, pieces of boiled meats served hot.

di **Gallina:** Boiled chicken.

di **Manzo:** Boiled beef.

Misto alla Piemontese: A mixed offering of boiled beef, pig's feet and head, veal shanks, sausages, chicken, and vegetables, served hot with an appropriate sauce (See Salsa Verde).

BOVE, Filetto di: Another name for beef, this is a filet.

BRACIOLE (INE): Should be a rib steak, with or without bone, cut from any of the eight ribs comprising the BRACIOLA, but can be cut from back into the loin.

alla **Fiorentina:** Same as Bistecca alla Fiorentina, a grilled rib steak of beef.

di **Maiale:** Pork cutlet or chop.

alla **Pizzaiola:** Grilled steak served with a sauce of garlic, tomatoes, parsley, and oregano in olive oil. (See Bistecca alla).

alla **Sassi:** Pork or beef steak fried, and served with small pieces of pan-fried potatoes. Sassi means stones or pebbles.

alla **Toscana:** Either grilled or broiled steak; or could be braised in a sauce of onion, white wine, or red wine, chopped raw ham, butter and olive oil, and served with garnish of boiled potatoes with garlic and nutmeg.

di **Vitello:** Veal steak.

BRACE (Alla): Charcoal broiled, or broiled over live coals.

BUE: Beef.

Costata di, alla Fiorentina: Another name for Bistecca alla Fiorentina - - charcoal broiled beef rib or T-bone steak.

Costata di, alla Tirolese: Grilled or broiled rib steak served with French-fried onion rings, or fried onions.

Costatella di, alla Maitre d'Hotel: Rib or T-bone steak, grilled, and served topped with a ball of creamed butter containing salt, pepper, chopped parsley and lemon juice.

BUE: (cont.)

> **Entrecote di:** Boneless rib steak of beef.

> **Fracosta di:** Another name for beef rib steak.

> **Sotto Filetto alla Bismark:** Boneless T-bone steak grilled and served with a fried egg on top.

> **Stracotto di, al Barolo:** Beef rib roast marinated in Barolo red wine, and pot-roasted in this marinade.

> **Stracotto di, con Peperonata:** Pot-roast of beef rib roast, with bell peppers in the cooking brew.

BUSECCA: (See Trippa alla Milanese).

CAPPONCELLO RUSPANTE al FORNO: Roast capon; Ruspante meaning « scratching », thus implying farm-raised or free-running.

CAPPONE: Capon, Petto di (breast of).

CAPRETTO: Baby goat.

> **Costolettine alla Brace:** Tiny ribs charcoal broiled.

> **Costolettine di, alla Milanese:** Tiny rib chops breaded and pan-fried golden in butter.

> al **Forno:** Roast young goat, usually with rosemary and sage, and basted with broth.

> alla **Pasqualina:** Traditional Italian Easter dinner meat dish, as we would have turkey for Thanksgiving; baby goat roasted in the oven with olive oil, carrots, onion, celery, sprigs of rosemary, black olives, and basted with white wine and broth.

> allo **Spiedo:** Young goat roasted on a spit.

CARBONATA: Basically a grilled pork cutlet, but in some areas could be a beef stew with sliced onions, red wine, and a touch of nutmeg.

CARNE FREDDA ASSORTITA: A plate of assorted cold meats, principally roasted and boiled ones.

CASTELLANA: Is really another name for a folded veal cutlet - - a thin slice of boneless veal, usually stuffed, and folded in half before being fried.

> alla **Marsala:** Veal cutlet covered with a slice of ham or Fontina cheese, folded, breaded, fried in butter and oil, and served in a sauce of pan juices and Marsala wine.

> al **Prosciutto:** Veal cutlet covered with slice of ham, folded, breaded, and served in brown sauce with pieces of chopped ham in it.

> **Tartufata:** The same, but served in a sauce of white wine and sliced truffles.

CASTRATO: Mutton, a castrated sheep.

> **Braciole di:** A mutton steak, or chops, rib or loin, grilled or fried.

CERVELLA: Brains, veal; in Rome could be of lamb.

al **Burro:** Brains, poached, sliced, floured, and fried golden in butter.

Dorate, al Tegamino: Brains, cut into pieces, floured, dipped in beaten egg, breaded, and fried golden in butter; served in small two-handled frying pan.

alla **Finanziera:** Poached, sliced, and served covered with a sauce flavored with truffles, or classically, served in a brown sauce containing tiny chicken dumplings, cockscombs, kidneys, olives, truffles, and mushrooms.

Fritto, Carciofi: Pieces of brains and artichokes breaded and fried golden.

Frittura di, con Mozzarella, Carciofi: Pieces of brains, Mozzarella cheese, and artichokes, breaded and deep-fried.

alla **Salvia:** Brains sautéed with sage leaves.

e **Zucchini:** Pieces of brains and zucchini squash breaded and fried golden.

CIMA: A specialty of Genoa - - lower breast meat (no bones) of veal stuffed with a paste of sweetbreads, bacon, onions, garlic, marjoram, cheese, peas, hard-boiled egg; simmered gently in broth of water, bay leaf, carrot, onion, celery. Then it is weighted and cooled, and served sliced, usually cold, and frequently with a cold herbal green sauce (See Salsa Verde). Weighting makes it bulge like a mountain top.

alla **Genovese:** The same as above.

di **Vitello:** The same, but the stuffing may vary.

CIMALINO di MANZO, FAGIOLI: A Cima cooked with dried beans in broth, and served with the beans.

CODA: Tail.

alla **Vaccinara:** Oxtail stewed in sauce of tomatoes, olive oil, garlic, white wine.

CONIGLIO: Rabbit, usually domestic.

alla **Cacciatora:** Hunter's style - - pieces browned in pork fat, braised in a gravy of shallots, white wine, tomato paste, and dried mushrooms.

Cosciotto di: Leg of rabbit; usually braised in an herbal gravy.

Farcito al Forno: Roasted stuffed rabbit - - stuffing of bread, cheese, garlic, lemon peel, oil, bacon, nutmeg, cinnamon, eggs and olive oil.

al **Forno:** Rabbit baked in the oven in sauce of rosemary, sage, onion, white wine and broth.

CONIGLIO: (cont.)

e **Polenta:** Braised or stewed pieces of rabbit served with a thick cornmeal mush on the side.

alla **Romagnola:** Pieces of rabbit marinated in herbal oil, dipped in egg, breaded, and fried in butter.

CONTROFILETTO alla BISMARK: Beef or veal loin steak fried, and served topped with a fried egg.

COSCIOTTO AGNELLO: Leg of lamb, roasted, or on a spit.

COSCIOTTO di PORCELLO al FORNO: Roasted leg of very young pig.

COSTA, COSTATA, COSTATE, COSTATELLA, COSTELLATA, COSTELLETA, COSTELLETINE, COSTOLETTA (E), COSTOLETTINE: All mean, in beef, a rib steak, and should be with bone in; in veal, lamb, or pork, can be cut as far back as to the T-bone steak.

alla **Bolognese:** A veal chop or cutlet marinated in lemon juice and grated Parmesan cheese; breaded, fried in butter, then covered with slice of Parmesan or Swiss cheese placed over slices of truffle, put under broiler to melt the cheese, and served with cooking butter poured over it, or a meat sauce. Can be done this way with lamb chops also.

di **Bue:** Beef rib steak.

Disossata: Boned rib steak.

alla **Fiorentina:** Charcoal broiled rib steak (See Bistecca alla Fiorentina).

Fritto di, con Funghi: Fried rib steak served topped with braised mushrooms.

alla **Maitre d'Hotel:** Rib or T-bone steak grilled and served topped with a ball of creamed butter containing salt, pepper, parsley and lemon juice.

di **Manzo:** Beef rib steak.

alla **Milanese:** The classical Milan preparation - - veal steak, bone in, rolled in flour, dipped in beaten egg, then rolled in bread-crumbs and grated Parmesan, and fried golden in butter. Served topped with chopped parsley and a slice of lemon.

alla **Parmigiana:** Fried veal rib steak served covered with melted shaved slices of Parmesan or Fontina cheese.

alla **Pizzaiola:** Veal rib steak, partly fried in oil, and finished cooking in a sauce of garlic, tomato paste and oregano.

al **Prosciutto:** A veal rib steak covered with slice of ham, breaded and fried. Then ham side covered with

COSTA: (cont.)

   al **Prosciutto:** (cont.)
   slice of cheese, and put under broiler. May have truffle slices and meat sauce over it.

   alla **Salvia:** Veal rib steak braised in Marsala wine and broth, and just before serving is sprinkled with sage leaves and grated Parmesan cheese.

   al **Soave:** Veal steak braised in Soave white wine.

   alla **Tirolese:** Grilled or broiled veal steak served with fried or French-fried onion rings.

   alla **Trifola:** Fried veal steak served in a sauce from pan juices with sliced truffles in it.

   alla **Valdostana:** Valley of Aosta style - - veal chop with a slice of Fontina cheese laid in a pocket cut into it, breaded, and fried golden in butter.

   alla **Zingara:** Gypsy style - - veal chop floured, fried in butter with Marsala wine, mushrooms, basil, parsley, and pieces of pickled tongue, and served in this sauce; or, a rib steak of veal served in a sauce of sliced bell peppers, dried mushrooms, onion, black olives, capers, sliced dill pickles, and tomatoes.

COTEGHINO (CCHINO): A relatively large seasoned pork sausage, raw, which is boiled in herbal broth and served hot.

   di **Cremona:** Same, but from town of Cremona.

   di **Modena:** Same, but from town of Modena, and the most famous of these.

COTOLETTA (E) (INE): A word used by chefs interchangeably with COSTOLETTA. Is usually a steak without bone, but may be cut even from the leg.

   alla **Bolognese:** See Costoletta. Is usually a steak as above.

   Carpionata: Veal chop, floured, fried, then marinated in herbal vinegar and served cold.

   alla **Milanese:** (See Costoletta above).

   alla **Petroniana:** Veal chop marinated in lemon juice and Parmesan cheese; breaded, fried, then covered with slice of ham and cream-onion sauce, and browned in the oven.

   al **Prosciutto:** (See Costoletta, above).

   Ripiena: A veal steak cut with horizontal pocket in it, which is stuffed with herbal and seasoned ground meat; floured, and fried golden.

CROCCHETTE: Croquettes.

   Cervella, Zucchini Fritti: Croquettes of brains and zucchini squash, breaded and deep-fried.

CROCCHETTE: (cont.)

di **Pollo:** Chicken croquettes, usually deep-fried.

DINDO: Turkey.

ENTRECOTE: Boneless rib steak of beef or veal.

alla **Bismark:** Rib steak fried in butter and oil, and served with fried egg on top.

alla **Pizzaiola:** Fried in oil and served in a garlic, oregano, tomato sauce.

alla **Tirolese:** Fried or grilled, and served covered with French-fried onion rings, or fried onions. May also have in addition, fried sliced tomato.

FAGIOLI co' le COTICHE: Dry, large white beans cooked with ham and pork skin, garlic, onions in a tomato sauce.

FARAONA: Guinea fowl.

all'**Arancio:** Pieces of guinea fowl braised in white wine and broth, with sage leaves, onion, grated orange peel, and served covered with sauce made from the pan drippings and juices, with chopped orange in it.

al **Cartoccio:** Pieces sautéed in oil and butter, and then spread with paste of bread crumbs, minced liver, herbs; sealed in oiled paper and baked in the oven.

Lardellata alla Fiamma: Guinea fowl with strips of pork fat threaded through the breast, and then spit-roasted.

all'**Oliva:** Pieces braised in oil and herbs with green or black olives.

FARSUMAGRU: Breast of veal stuffed with hard-boiled eggs, cheese, raw ham, chopped sausage, garlic, parsley, and roasted in oil, garlic, and whole sprigs of parsley. Can also be a large, thin round steak with these ingredients spread on, then rolled, tied firm and roasted, as above, or braised with onion, tomato paste, water. Can be eaten either hot or cold, sliced.

FEGATELLI: Pork liver, or pork liver pieces.

alla **Fiorentina:** Pieces of pork liver rolled in bread crumbs containing slivered garlic, fennel seeds, then wrapped with pork caul fat (a delicate network or lacework of fat from around the pork stomach), then skewered with alternating sage leaf, bread round, and liver, and oven-cooked in a pan with olive oil.

Fricando con Rete allo Spiedo: Pieces of pork liver rolled in herbal bread crumbs, wrapped with Rete (the lacework of fat covering pork stomach), skewered, and oven or spit-roasted.

FEGATINI: Liver, implying small ones, or small pieces - usually meaning chicken livers, if not otherwise designated.

di **Maiale:** Small pieces of pork liver. This could be braised in white wine and bay leaf, fried with onions, or braised in tomatoes, lard, onions. There are various preparations.

di **Pollo, al Burro e Salvia:** Chicken livers fried in butter with sage leaves.

FEGATO: Liver, and when not explained, would mean calf or beef liver.

al **Burro:** Sliced calf's liver fried in butter - - may be floured first.

alla **Fiorentina:** Florence style - - floured, cooked in olive oil with fresh sage, garlic, tomato paste.

• **Lame di:** Slices of liver.

alla **Salvia:** Fried (usually breaded) sliced veal liver, served in butter in which fresh sage has been braised.

alla **Veneta:** Usually means same as alla Veneziana - - liver and onions.

alla **Veneziana:** The well-known Venice preparation of sliced calf liver cooked in olive oil with sliced onions, served with lemon juice over.

di **Vitello:** Calf's liver, usually called Fegato di Vitello, then « alla this or that ».

FERRI (Ai): Literally « on iron ». Means grilled on a ridged, or flat steel plate.

FESA: Top round steak, a ligament stripped lengthwise from veal leg, then sliced across the grain, making a small diameter piece of round steak.

Arrosto: Roast top round of veal, or if « Morto », is pot-roasted.

al **Forno:** Roast top round of veal, baked in the oven.

con **Funghi Freschi e Piselli:** Top round of veal pot-roasted with herbs, mushrooms, and peas.

Glassata: Roast of veal either glazed, or served sliced with a transluscent sauce of herbs, pan juices.

al **Vino Bianco:** Slices of roast round of veal served in a sauce made with pan juices and white wine, or could simply be fried slices served in this sauce.

FILETTO di BUE, di MANZO (or simply FILETTO): Beef filet or tenderloin, or filet mignon, all meaning the same.

alla **Bismark:** Grilled or fried tenderloin steak served topped with a fried egg.

69

FILETTO di BUE: (cont.)

alla **Bolognese:** Fried tenderloin steak; then covered with slice of Fontina cheese or Parmesan cheese, or slice of ham, and put under broiler, or fried in a sauce of Marsala wine and grated Parmesan cheese.

alla **Brace di Legno:** Broiled over wood coals.

alla **Contadina:** Peasant woman style - - tenderloin steaks in which a pocket is made and stuffed with a mixture of capers, olives, and anchovy; fried, and then braised in onion sauce with tomato paste and butter.

alla **Fiamma:** Charcoal broiled.

al **Marsala:** Fried or grilled and served in a sauce of pan juices, onion, Marsala wine.

al **Rossini:** Tenderloin steak slices served fried or grilled with slice of goose liver topped with slice of truffle.

Sotto Filetto Farcito: Beef loin steak stuffed with herbal ground meat, roasted or braised.

Tartara: Raw ground filet steak served with raw egg folded in, and garnished with capers, chopped onions, anchovies.

FOIOLO: Tripe, the stomach lining of beef or veal.

alla **Bolognese:** Veal tripe braised or stewed in a tomato sauce with garlic, white wine, vinegar, and with grated Parmesan cheese.

alla **Genovese:** Tripe cooked in herbal tomato sauce, rosemary, onion, white wine, and served with grated Parmesan cheese.

alla **Milanese:** Tripe braised in white wine, onion, celery, carrots and herbs.

al **Sugo:** In a sauce of onion, tomato and herbs.

FRACOSTA alla GRIGLIA: This is a rib steak grilled.

FRICANDO: Bottom round of veal or baby beef.

GALLINA: A name for chicken.

Bollita Padovana: Boiled chicken from Padua.

GESUITA al MADERA: Last cut of rib steak forward, high on shoulder of the animal. So-called in implying the reversed collar of a Jesuit priest, this one being served in a Madeira wine sauce.

GIAMBONETTE: Meaning a little leg, is usually a boned chicken leg and thigh, stuffed with chicken, ham, bacon, garlic, thyme, egg, Parmesan cheese, and parsley, then fried, or braised in broth, and served with a number of different sauces.

GIAMBONETTE: (cont.)

Delizia con Pisellini: « Delight », the boned stuffed chicken leg served with small peas, either fresh or canned.

di **Pollo e Pisellini:** Of chicken, served with peas.

Tartufato: Braised and served in sauce with slices of truffle or with truffle essence.

GIRELLO (INE) di VITELLO: The Girello is one of the ligaments of the leg of veal or beef which is stripped out lengthwise from the leg, then roasted whole or sliced. It is actually a round steak of veal. You encounter it so often by its name, that it is translated here rather than under VITELLO (veal).

al **Forno:** Roundsteak roast of veal.

alla **Genovese:** Slices of veal round steak roast served in a sauce Salsa Verde, of olive oil, capers, filets of anchovy, bread soaked in vinegar, and lots of chopped parsley. Usually served cold.

al **Madera:** Veal round steak fried or braised in butter and Madeira wine, and served with sauce from pan juices and more Madeira wine.

al **Soave:** Slices fried or braised in butter and white Soave wine, as with Madeira.

al **Vino Bianco:** Same as with Soave, but using another white wine.

GOULASCH alla UNGHERESE: Hungarian Goulash - - veal or beef chunks braised in a mild red Paprika sauce.

GRANATINA: Is the same as Steak Tartare - - ground raw beef served with various condiments and sauces. May be called « alla LUCULLO ».

GRIGLIA (Alla): Cooked on a grill. Grilled.

GRIGLIATA MISTA: A mixed grill; chops, steak, perhaps some liver, grilled.

HASCE di MANZO al BURRO: Hamburger patty fried in butter.

INVOLTINI: These are thin slices of veal spread with a paste or stuffing of various ingredients, such as chopped herbs, ham, etc., and rolled up, then braised in butter and oil, i.e., veal rolls stuffed. Can be of ham or pork.

al **Cognac:** Veal rolls stuffed with chopped mushrooms, truffles, bread crumbs, in egg binder, cooked in butter, then flamed in cognac brandy, with pan juices poured over the veal rolls when served.

alla **Groviera:** Veal rolls with Gruyere (Swiss cheese) inside, cooked in butter and served in a very thin tomato sauce.

INVOLTINI: (cont.)

di **Pollo al Prosciutto:** Breast of chicken rolled around slices of cooked ham, floured, butter-fried, and served with a sauce of pan juices, white wine and chopped ham.

al **Prosciutto:** With chopped ham in the stuffing.

LAMELLE FEGATO: Very thin slices of veal or beef liver, usually sautéed in butter.

LINGUA di BUE, di VITELLO: Beef, veal tongue.

alla **Fiamminga:** Beef tongue Flemish style; braised in gravy of beer, onion, broth, mushrooms and herbs.

alla **Parmigiana:** Parma style; slices of boiled tongue covered with slices of Parmesan cheese, melted in oven and served hot.

al **Pomodoro:** Boiled tongue slices, re-heated in herbal tomato sauce.

e **Prosciutto al Madera:** Slices of tongue and ham served in a Madeira wine sauce.

Salmistrata: Pickled beef tongue usually served cold with a sauce on the side.

di **Vitello e Salsa Verde:** Slices of boiled veal tongue served cold in a green sauce of capers, olive oil, anchovies, chopped parsley.

LOMBATA (O) (INA) (E) di VITELLO: Loin of veal (or beef). The loin part from which comes the T-bone steak, but without bone. Is spelled several ways, such as LOMBO, LOMATA, etc.

con **Funghi:** Sautéed veal loin steak served covered with mushroom sauce of pan juices.

alla **Pizzaiola:** Thin slices served sautéed in a sauce of tomato, garlic, oregano, oil, capers.

alla **Salvia:** Slices floured, sautéed in butter with several sage leaves on top.

alla **Sassi:** Steak floured, sautéed in butter with leaves of sage on top, and served with little pebble-sized pieces of fried potatoes.

LONZA: Loin, usually of pork.

LUGANEGA con PISELLI: Shoulder of pork, ground, mixed with Parmesan cheese, put into pork sausage casing, served fried hot, in this case with peas on the side.

LUMACHE: Snails.

alla **Bourguignonne:** Burgundy snails - - snails, washed, cooked, removed from the shells, scrubbed, returned to shells which are sealed over with garlic butter. Served bubbling hot from the oven with bread to sop up the melted butter out of each shell.

LUMACHE: (cont.)

    alla **Parigina:** Snails served same as Bourguignonne, above.

    alla **Romana:** Snails braised in their shells in a sauce of tomatoes, anchovies, mint leaves, garlic and olive oil.

    alla **Valdostana:** Braised in their shells in a tomato sauce with garlic, olive oil, mushrooms and herbs.

MAGRO di VITELLO: Lean veal meat, could be any cut as long as it is lean.

MAIALE: Pork.

    Arista di Maiale: Roast saddle or loin of pork with or without bone in. If « alla Fiorentina » or « alla Toscana », is the well-known Tuscany preparation; rubbed with, or having stuck into it a paste of garlic, rosemary, cloves, salt and pepper; roasted in oven, or turned on a spit.

    Arrostetti: Small roast of pork.

    Arrostino alla Salvia: Small pork roast with sage leaves on it, and basted with broth and minced vegetables while roasting.

    Arrosto in Porchetta: Roast suckling pig, or in Southern Adriatic area, can be a larger pig stuffed with herbs such as rosemary, wild fennel and garlic, bacon, salt and pepper, and the pìg's liver. This may be spit-roasted.

    Carre di: Roast loin or saddle of pork.

    Costolette di: Pork chop.

    alla **Sassi Marconi:** Pork chops, stuffed with a layer of Fontina cheese, ham, then breaded and fried in oil.

    Fegatini: Pork liver, braised in white wine and bay leaf, fried with onions, or braised in tomatoes, lard, onions, and there are also other preparations.

    Lombo or Lombata: Roast loin of pork, or fried or sautéed slices of loin.

    Lonza di Maiale: Another name for loin of pork.

    Nodini alla Griglia: Grilled little pork steaks from the tenderloin or loin.

    alla **Pizzaiola:** Slices of pork loin or tenderloin braised in a sauce of capers, tomatoes, garlic, oregano, oil, butter and parsley.

    Spuntatura di, Polenta: Short ribs or breast of pork served with a thick cornmeal mush.

    Zampe di Maiale (Cotta al Vapore): Pig's feet boiled in herbal broth.

MANZO: A steer, or castrated beef.

MANZO: (cont.)

Battuto di: Ground beef, or hamburger. Would be sautéed or fried.

Bistecca di: Beefsteak.

Bollito: Boiled beef - - simmered in herbal broth.

Brasato (Con Peperonata): Pot roast of beef, in this case including bell peppers among other ingredients.

Cestata di: Rib steak of beef.

Cimalino di: Boiled stuffed breast of beef (e Fagioli) - - served with dried beans cooked in same broth as the beef.

Costata (e) di: Steer rib steak.

Costata Disossata: Boned beef rib steak, a Spencer or Delmonico or Market steak.

Fracosta di: Another name for rib steak.

Lesso: Boiled steer beef.

Pastissa con Funghi: Beef pot pie with pastry on top, and containing mushrooms in the sauce or gravy.

Polpette di: Meat balls of beef, usually cooked in an herbal gravy.

Stracotto di: Beef pot roast.

MEDAGLIONE: These are little round discs of steak cut from tenderloin, loin, sirloin, or round of veal.

al **Barolo:** Braised in, and served in a sauce of Barolo red wine.

di **Bue alla Provinciale:** Beef medallion steaks fried, served in a sauce of brains, sweetbreads and peas, broth and herbs.

al **Madera:** Fried, and then Madeira wine added in the finishing of the cooking. Meat removed, and a sauce made of pan juices and Madeira wine, slightly thickened, and poured over steaks.

alla **Primavera:** Steaks, fried, and served in a thin sauce of mushrooms, parsley, onion, and a touch of tomato. Usually garnished with a collection of cooked fresh vegetables.

di **Vitello Zingaretta:** Veal tenderloin steaks Gypsy style; served covered with a brown sauce or gravy of tomato, onions, mushrooms, pickled tongue slices, truffles and paprika.

MESSICANI: Involtini or veal rolls - - thin slices of round steak (Fesa) of veal wrapped around a mixture of ground Prosciutto (ham), pork, chicken livers, parsley, sage

MESSICANI: (cont.)

egg, grated Parmesan cheese, white wine, butter and oil, sautéed and served in sauce of pan juices.

alla **Milanese:** Thin veal cutlets rolled, stuffed with ground meat mixture of ham, pork, garlic, Parmesan cheese, nutmeg; then floured, braised in white wine and broth, with rice put in at end, and served with the rice.

alla **Villereccia:** These veal rolls, stuffed as above, are braised in and served in a sauce of mushrooms, chopped vegetables, including bell peppers.

MISTO (I): Meaning mixed, a serving of various cuts or pieces of meat.

di **Arrosto di Vitello:** Pieces or slices of roast veal.

Griglia Carne or alla Griglia: A mixed grill of various cuts and pieces of grilled meat, usually veal.

Rifreddo: Cold cooked mixed meats; usually roasted or spit-turned, and often served in a cold sauce, such as a grated tuna-mayonnaise sauce - - Tonnato.

MONTONE: Mutton.

MOSTARDA di FRUTTA: A specialty of Cremona which consists of various preserved fruits in a mustard sauce, served with cold meats or chicken.

MOZZARELLA: A mild stringy cheese most notably made from water buffalo milk.

Bufalo: Stressing the fact that it is made of water buffalo milk, usually pear-shaped ball, waxy and rubbery in consistancy, and mostly used in cooking.

in **Carrozza:** A slice of Mozzarella cheese put between two slices of bread, dipped in beaten egg, breaded, and then deep-fried.

Crostini di: Slices of Mozzarella cheese and slices of bread alternating on a skewer; then put in the oven (al Forno), for cheese to melt, and served with a melted butter and anchovy sauce.

alla **Milanese:** Slice of Mozzarella cheese dipped in batter and bread crumbs and deep-fried, or only in flour and not bread crumbs, and deep-fried.

alla **Romana:** Thick slice of this cheese breaded and fried golden.

Spiedini: Same as Crostini - - skewered alternating pieces of cheese and bread, baked in the oven, served with melted butter and anchovy sauce.

NOCE: Top round of veal.

NODINO di VITELLO: These are, or can be the same as Medaglione, that is, small disc-shaped steaks usually of veal, taken from the tenderloin (filet), or cut from the loin, or top sirloin, or even the round.

al **Burro e Salvia:** Fried in butter with sage leaves on the steaks.

alla **Panna:** Floured, fried in butter, and finished cooking in, and served in a cream sauce with onions and mushrooms in it.

alla **Pizzaiola:** Fried, and covered with a sauce of pan juices, garlic, tomato, oil and oregano.

alla **Sassi:** Floured, fried, then braised in white wine with sage leaves, served with Rissole (pan-roasted) potatoes, pebble-size.

al **Vino Soave:** Fried, then braised in sauce of herbs and white Soave wine.

OSSOBUCO (CHI): This is a piece of veal shank cut across the bone, horizontally.

con **Funghi:** Stewed or braised, then served in gravy to which mushrooms have been added.

alla **Gremolada (also Cremolata):** Same as alla Milanese, but at end of cooking, slightly-cooked grated lemon peel, sage leaves, cloves of garlic, chopped parsley are added and then gravy poured over the meat when served.

alla **Lombarda:** Braised, then floured, fried in butter; served with lemon juice and chopped parsley.

alla **Milanese:** Braised in white wine, broth, tomato, and at end some grated lemon peel and chopped parsley added.

con **Purea:** Braised, sliced, and served on, or with mashed potatoes.

al **Vino Bianco:** Braised in white wine and broth; served with a slice of garlic on top and sprinkled with grated lemon peel and chopped parsley.

PAIATA (PAETA) al MALGARAGNO: Hen turkey spit-roasted and basted with drippings and pomegranite juice, and served in sauce of these liquids.

PAILLARD: Technically is a beef rib steak, but currently the name is applied to a veal cutlet of large diameter, pounded thin, and served grilled.

alla **Piastra:** Grilled on a flat steel plate.

PECORA, il FIGLIO della PECORA: Literally, the son of a ewe, i.e., a baby sheep.

Pasqualina: Easter style -- a renowned preparation at Easter time -- roasted in oven with olive oil, carrots,

PECORA, il FIGLIO della PECORA: (cont.)
    Pasqualina: (cont.)
celery, onion, rosemary, garlic and black olives. There
are several variations on this preparation. Usually done
with baby goat (Capretto).

PETTO di POLLO: Breast of chicken. Also PETTICINI.
Many preparations.

all'**Arancio:** Sautéed in brown sauce with orange
juice and grated orange flavoring it.

alla **Bolognese:** Bologna style - - floured, egg-dipped,
fried in butter, covered with slice of ham, Fontina cheese,
put under broiler and served with pan juices, and a line
of meat sauce dribbled over it.

al **Burro:** Floured, fried in butter, then finished by
braising in the oven, and served with cooking juices
poured over it.

    Crema e Funghi: Braised in butter and lemon
juice, finally steeped in cream sauce with mushrooms,
white wine, fresh basil, and chopped parsley.

    Disossato al Prosciutto: Boned breast of chicken,
breaded and fried; then covered with slice of ham, sprinkled with grated Parmesan cheese and put in the oven. Can
be decorated with touch of tomato paste, chopped parsley.

    Dorato (i): Floured, egg-dipped, breaded, fried
golden, or braised in oil in the oven.

con **Funghi:** Floured, fried, then braised in the oven
in butter, and served with sliced mushrooms, or in a
mushroom cream sauce.

alla **Milanese:** Milan style; floured, egg-dipped, breaded
and fried golden.

alla **Panna:** Braised in butter with lemon juice, finally
steeped in cream sauce, usually containing mushrooms
or truffles, or both, and white wine and basil.

alla **Parigina:** Parisian style; fried in butter, finished by
braising in oven, served covered with rich mushroom
cream sauce.

alla **Princessa:** Floured, fried golden in butter and
served with fried egg on top.

al **Prosciutto:** First breaded and fried, then covered
with slice of cooked ham, sprinkled with grated Parmesan
cheese, put under broiler, decorated with chopped parsley,
and possibly tomato paste.

al **Vino Bianco:** In white wine; floured, fried in butter
and bathed in white wine. Served in a sauce made from
pan juices and more white wine.

PIACERE (a): Of your choice, the way you like it served.

PICCATA (INA): These are small-sized veal cutlets. Usually 3 or 4 are served, thin and tiny.

all'**Allegro:** Same as alla Lombarda, but with no parsley.

ai **Capperi:** Fried in butter, and served with capers and herbs in pan juices.

Dorata: Floured, dipped in beaten egg, and fried golden.

al **Limone:** Same as alla Lombarda.

alla **Lombarda:** Lombardy style; fried in butter, and when nearly done, lemon juice and chopped parsley are added. Served with pan juices poured over.

al **Madera:** Gently fried, then braised, and served in a sauce of pan juices to which Madeira wine has been added.

PICCIONE (CINO): Means pigeon, but also is the name for one ligament in a round steak.

in **Casseruola:** Pigeon, cut up, braised in sauce of Marsala wine, butter, broth, mushrooms, onion. Many variations of this dish.

alla **Fiorentina:** Pigeon, stuffed inside with bay leaf, bacon, small potato, and dusted with nutmeg. Browned in butter, sage and oil, and braised in the oven and served on rice cooked in milk, with grated Parmesan cheese mixed in.

alle **Mele:** Roasted pigeon served with applesauce.

PIZZAIOLA di MANZO: Fried or grilled T-bone or sirloin steak of beef served covered with sauce made from pan juices, olive oil, garlic, tomato and oregano.

POLLO: This is chicken, and it has many names, such as GALLINA, POLLASTRA (hen 7-8 months old): POLLASTRO (chicken 3-4 months old): POLLASTRELLO (boiling chicken): POLLASTRINO (implying a small chicken).

all'**Arancio:** In orange; roasted or braised chicken served in a sauce of pan juices, arrowroot thickened, and with orange juice and grated orange peel in it. Served garnished with orange slices.

Arrosto: Roast chicken.

in **Bellavista:** Roasted, served on fried bread, and with an artistic assembly of various cooked vegetables as garnish.

Bollito: Boiled chicken.

alla **Cacciatora:** Hunter's style; there are many variations of this, but basically it is in pieces, browned in oil and lard, then braised in onion, herbs, white wine (or red), and with or without tomatoes and mushrooms.

POLLO: (cont.)

alla **Casalinga:** Home style - - could be any preparation, but is usually a variation of alla Cacciatora.

al **Chianti:** Braised or stewed in Chianti red wine and herbs, onion, etc., much the same as the French « Coq au Vin Rouge ».

Costolettine di, Pomodoro, Funghi: Breast of chicken braised and served in sauce of tomato and mushrooms.

Crochetta (ine): Chicken croquettes, fried or deep-fried.

alla **Diavola:** Simply a broiler, basted with oil while being grilled (flattened), or broiled over coals, or on a spit, possibly with a slight touch of cayenne pepper in the basting oil.

Farcito Tartufato: Boned, roasted with stuffing of spinach, peas, truffles, parsley, cooked ham and grated cheese.

Fegatini di: Chicken livers usually sautéed in butter.

al **Forno:** Roast chicken.

Fritto alla Toscana: Fried chicken Tuscany style; split, marinated in oil, lemon juice and parsley; then floured, dipped in beaten egg, and fried golden in oil. Or, floured, fried in olive oil, finished frying in oil with chopped artichokes. Beaten egg and lemon juice then added. Served when the egg is cooked.

Fritto Fiorentina: Fried Florence style; pieces marinated in oil, lemon juice and herbs, then fried golden in olive oil. Served with chopped parsley and a slice of lemon. But, may also be floured, dipped in beaten egg before being fried.

Giambonette di: Boned leg and thigh of chicken stuffed with ham, chicken, bacon, garlic, thyme, egg, grated Parmesan cheese; fried, then served in any number of sauces, and also with peas, truffles, etc.

al **Girarrosto:** Turned on a spit; spit-roasted.

Glassato: Roasted or sautéed, and served in an arrowroot thickened sauce. Or, can be cold roast chicken glazed with aspic, served with fancy garnish.

all'**Indiana:** Chicken curry or curried chicken, i.e., Indian style.

Lesso (ato): Boiled chicken (con Bietole) - - simmered in vegetable broth with Swiss chard, and served on a bed of the chard.

POLLO: (cont.)

alla **Marengo:** A renowned dish, but 7 books will give 7 recipes. It was served to Napoleon after his victory over the Austrians at Marengo in 1800. His chef, scrambling for ingredients came up with sautéed chicken in olive oil with tomatoes, garlic, fresh water crayfish steamed over the cooking chicken, and some fried eggs placed on fried bread, surrounding the dish as a garnish. Now it is usually served in a brown gravy with mushrooms, perhaps truffes, with or without tomatoes, and surrounded with fried eggs on fried bread, and garnished with boiled crayfish or shrimps.

alla **Marescialla:** Boneless chicken fried in butter, perhaps floured and egg-dipped.

alla **Montanara:** Garlic-rubbed, rosemary stuffed, braised in olive oil, onion, butter, juniper sticks, grape brandy and broth.

Nostrale, Nostrano: Meaning of our region, or grown locally.

Novello: Meaning new or young.

Petto di: Breast of chicken, see Petto (many preparations).

Raspante: Scratching, implying farm-raised.

Rigaglie di, alla Salvia: Chicken giblets, in this case, with sage - - the livers and other parts sautéed with sage leaves.

alla **Romana:** Roman style; cut in pieces, browned in pork fat and bacon with garlic. Cooking finished with addition of white wine and tomato paste, hot water, sliced bell peppers, and braised until done.

Rosmarino: Roasted with sprigs of rosemary in the cavity.

Schiacciato: Grilled halves or quarters with slices of bacon, and served with the pieces of bacon over the chicken.

Sott'Aceti: Literally « under vinegar »; roasted and served with a garnish of little vinegar pickles, onions, olives.

alla **Spezzatino:** Little pieces. See Spezzatine. It is braised pieces in tomato, broth and herbs. There are many preparations of this.

allo **Spiedo:** Broiled on a spit, or skewered and cooked in the oven.

in **Umido alla Casalinga:** Braised or stewed in broth with onion, carrot, celery, tomatoes, oil, parsley, herbs. Casalinga means home style.

POLPETTA (E) (INE): Meat balls. Also called PORPETTE.

    Cassarecce: From Rome, meaning home style - - meat balls in tomato sauce.

  con **Fagioli:** Meat balls served with boiled dried white beans.

  di **Manzo:** Of beef.

  al **Sugo:** Should be meat balls served in an herbal tomato sauce, but can be stuffed with cheese and sausage, breaded and deep-fried.

POLPETTONE: A veal roll, flavored with ham, cheese, herbs, or for FARCITO a SORPRESA, is a veal-beef meat loaf with onion, garlic, Parmesan cheese, oil, salt and pepper, tomato paste.

PORCELLO, COSCIOTTO di, al FORNO: Very young pig, in this case roasted leg of pork.

PORCHETTA: Suckling pig.

  al **Forno:** Roast suckling pig.

PORTAFOGLIO: A thin veal cutlet usually spread with, or stuffed with a ground meat mixture with herbs, ham, perhaps slice of cheese, folded, pinned and then fried or braised in a sauce or oil.

    Farcito: Stuffed.

    Imbottito: Also means stuffed.

PROSCIUTTO: The Italian word for ham. Can be either cooked (COTTO), or raw (CRUDO), the latter being salted, air-dried and aged for a long time. A highly prized delicacy in Italy.

  al **Madera:** Slices of cooked ham served in a brown sauce made with Madeira wine.

PUNTA di VITELLO: Plate or brisket breast of veal, usually roasted.

QUAGLIE: Quail (See CACCIAGIONE - - wild game, next section).

RANE (RANNOCCHI): Frogs' legs, or can be whole frogs rather than just the legs.

RIGAGLIA (E): Giblets, usually of chicken.

ROGNONE: Kidneys, usually veal, but may be di MAIALE.

    Funghi Trifolati: Floured, fried in butter, and braised in a broth with garlic, chopped mushrooms, parsley.

  al **Madera:** Sliced veal kidneys floured, braised in butter and Madeira wine, and served in a sauce made of pan juices and more Madeira wine.

    Maitre d'Hotel: Whole veal kidneys grilled, basted with butter, and served on a bed of butter creamed with chopped parsley and lemon juice.

PIATTI del GIORNO

ROGNONE: (cont.)

Trifolato: Sliced, floured, fried in butter and oil, garlic, sprinkled with chopped parsley, served with a squeeze of lemon juice.

ROLLATINE di VITELLO: Small veal cutlets usually rolled around some stuffing of ham, or cheese, and either fried, or sautéed in a sauce.

SALSA: Sauce.

SALSA VERDE: A green sauce of chopped parsley, capers, anchovies, dill pickles, bread, garlic, onion, vinegar, olive oil; served cold.

SALSICCIA: Sausage. Fresh sausage usually, which must be cooked.

Fritto: Fried sausage.

al **Sugo:** Fresh pork sausages fried, then braised and served in a meat sauce or gravy.

di **Treviso e Polenta:** Fresh pork sausage from Treviso, fried, and served with a slice of thick cornmeal mush.

SALTIMBOCCA: These are the same as Scaloppine, or are thin cutlets of veal.

alla **Romana:** Thin slices of veal with a fresh sage leaf, then covered with a slice of ham and fried in butter, with possibly white wine added in the frying.

SANATO: Very young calf which has never had solid food.

SCALOPPINE, SCALOPPA (E): Probably the most frequently encoutered meat dish offered in Italy. It is no more than a boneless, thin slice of meat, usually veal, and can come from nearly any part of the animal, the choicest being from the loin, tenderloin, sirloin and round. There seem to be an infinite number of ways of preparing this cut of meat, and variations will be found even though the dish will be listed with the same name.

all'**Arancio:** Sautéed in butter and oil, then orange juice and grated orange peel is added to the pan juices to make the sauce.

alla **Bismark:** Fried in butter and served with a fried egg on top.

alla **Bolognese:** Bologna style; breaded, fried golden, covered with a slice of ham and of Parmesan cheese which is oven-melted. May be served topped with a meat sauce.

alla **Boscaiola:** Woodsman's style; sautéed in oil and butter and served in a sauce of onion, black olives, rosemary, mushrooms, and topped with bits of tomato, and put under the broiler.

SCALOPPINE, SCALOPPA (E): (cont.)

al **Burro:** Floured, fried in butter, with browned butter poured over in serving.

alla **Cacciatora:** Hunter's style; fried in butter and served in tomato sauce with thyme, bay leaf, parsley, mushrooms, capers and black olives.

alla **Campagnola:** Rural or rustic style; same as alla Boscaiola, but with also celery and carrot in the sauce.

alla **Capricciosa:** Fried, or sautéed in a mushroom sauce with chopped ham, shallots, garlic, oregano, and served with a pattern of ham strips and strips of melted cheese.

alla **Contadina:** Peasant woman style; sautéed, and served in a tomato sauce with chopped olives, capers, grated Parmesan cheese, and onion.

alla **Crema:** Sautéed and served in a white cream sauce.

alla **Crema con Funghi:** Same as alla Crema, but with mushrooms in the sauce.

Cremata: Sautéed and served in a white cream sauce containing also egg yolk and cognac.

al **Formaggio:** Fried, and covered with slice of cheese, melted in the oven.

al **Funghetto:** A way of cooking; sautéed in very hot oil with rosemary, sage, garlic, and bathed with white wine.

con **Funghi:** Browned in butter, then grilled, and served in a mushroom cream sauce.

alla **Guarienti (or Guarnite):** Sautéed, and served with some special garnish.

al **Limone:** Marinated in lemon juice and garlic, and sautéed in oil and the marinade.

alla **Lombarda:** Sautéed in oil and butter with lemon juice and chopped parsley added.

al **Madera:** Fried in oil, butter and Madeira wine, and served in sauce made from pan juices and additional Madeira with some thickening.

al **Marsala:** Fried in oil and butter and served in a sauce made from pan juices and the sweet, amber-coloured, fortified, Marsala wine.

alla **Milanese:** Rolled in flour, dipped in beaten egg, then in bread crumbs and grated Parmesan cheese, and fried golden; served topped with slice of lemon and chopped parsley.

alla **Panna:** Fried in butter, and served in a gravy of cream with lemon juice, and possibly mushrooms.

SCALOPPINE, SCALOPPA (E): (cont.)

alla **Panna Funghetto:** Same as Funghetto, but with cream added at last minute.

alla **Parmigiana:** Parma style - - dipped in beaten egg, rolled in grated Parmesan cheese and bread crumbs, and fried golden; or breaded, fried, and served topped with a slice of Parmesan or Fontina cheese melted under the broiler.

alla **Petroniana:** Marinated in lemon juice and grated Parmesan cheese, breaded, fried, served covered with cream onion sauce and a slice of ham; browned under the broiler. Or, floured, fried in butter and Marsala wine, topped with a slice of white truffle, grated Parmesan cheese, then braised in the oven in broth, served with colorful vegetable garnish.

Piccante: Braised in butter and oil, with garlic; doused with brandy, and for final cooking, the addition of a paste of anchovy, parsley, basil and capers spread on the meat.

Piccate: Three or four very small cutlets per person, sautéed and served in pan juices.

con **Piselli:** Sautéed in butter, and served covered with cooked peas.

alla **Pizzaiola:** Sautéed, and served in a sauce of pan juices, garlic, tomato, oil and oregano.

al **Pomodoro:** Sautéed; served in tomato sauce with herbs, topped with slice of cooked tomato.

al **Pomodoro e Funghi:** Same as al Pomodoro, but with mushrooms also in the sauce.

alla **Sorrentina:** Pan-fried in butter with beef concentrate, topped with slice of Mozzarella cheese and tomato sauce, and browned in the oven.

all'**Uccelletto:** Implying birds, or outdoors taste; sautéed in oil and butter, but with fresh sage leaves on the meat; used often in the preparation of wild game. May have a few drops of lemon juice squeezed on.

alla **Valdostana:** Valley of Aosta style - - can be either a pocket cut into the cutlet, into which a slice of Fontina cheese is placed (and perhaps a slice of white truffle), then closed, breaded, and fried golden. Or, a slice of Fontina cheese on the cutlet, after frying, and then melted under the broiler. Or, breaded, fried golden, then slice of Fontina put on it and melted under broiler.

alla **Viennese:** Breaded, fried golden, topped with a touch of anchovy butter lying on a slice of lemon covered

SCALOPPINE, SCALOPPA (E): (cont.)

   alla **Viennese:** (cont.)

   with a mixture of chopped egg white, yolk, capers, and
   green olives, or possibly with a rolled anchovy filet on
   a slice of lemon.

   al **Vino Bianco:** Sautéed in butter having white wine
   poured into pan, and served in sauce made with pan
   juices, more white wine to deglaze the pan.

   alla **Zingara:** Gypsy style; floured, sautéed in butter
   with Marsala wine, mushrooms, basil, parsley, and pieces
   of pickled tongue, and served in this sauce. Or, sautéed
   and served in sauce of sliced bell peppers, dried
   mushrooms, onion, black olives, capers, sliced dill pickles
   and tomatoes.

SCANELLO: Sirloin, or round steak, or cutlet of veal or
   beef.

SOTTOFILETTO (FARCITO): Loin steak of veal or
   beef. In this case stuffed with herbal ground meat and
   roasted.

SOTTONOCE: Top round of veal, can be a piece roasted,
   or more frequently, a cutlet.

SPEZZATINO (I): A stew of cubed meat in a gravy or
   sauce. Braised, actually.

   alla **Contadina:** Peasant woman style; cubes of veal
   braised in a sauce of chopped olives, capers, anchovy,
   grated Parmesan cheese, onion, tomato paste, and broth.

   alla **Paesana:** Also peasant woman style; cubes of
   veal braised in a sauce as in alla Contadina, but probably with mushrooms in it as well.

   al **Prosciutto:** Veal cubes with chopped ham pieces
   stewed in an herbal tomato sauce with red wine.

SPEZZATO: Also a stew of braised veal or beef in a tomato
   sauce with onion, herbs, wine.

SPIEDINI: Pieces or cubes of meat skewered, and usually
   grilled or roasted in the oven.

   alla **Corsara Flambe:** Skewered meat served flaming
   with brandy.

SPIEDO (Allo): Roasted on a spit, or skewered and
   grilled.

SPUNTATURA (di): Short ribs or a breast of.

STRACOTTO: Another word for stew or braised pieces
   or cubes of meat.

   alla **Toscana:** Braised cubes of veal done in an herbal
   tomato gravy with red wine.

PIATTI
del GIORNO

85

STUFATINO: Still another word for a stew or pot-roast of veal or beef, done with herbs, wine, broth, probably also tomato.

TACCHINO: Turkey.

Arrosto di: Roast turkey.

Boscaiolo: Woodsman's style; turkey breast meat in a sauce with tongue, ham, and mushrooms with herbs.

Filetto di: Next to the breast bone, the underneath ligament of turkey breast meat.

Nostrano Arrosto: Meaning home or locally grown, roasted.

Petto di: Breast of turkey.

Polpettone di: A patty of ground turkey breast meat with herbs, grated cheese in it, breaded and fried golden.

al **Prosciutto:** Breast filet floured, fried golden, covered with a slice of ham, and a spoon of grated Parmesan cheese, placed under the broiler.

in **Salsa Reale:** Breast filet served in a thin cream sauce fortified with egg yolk and cognac.

TESTINA: Head, usually veal or calf head, normally simmered in stock.

e **Lingua Lessa:** Veal head and tongue boiled in an aromatic herbal broth.

di **Vitello:** Calf's head; again, usually removed from bone and boiled in stock.

TORTINO di CARCIOFI: Fried artichoke hearts mixed with beaten eggs and made into a thick, flat omelette.

TOURNEDOS: Beef or veal tenderloin (filet) steak.

al **Barolo:** Fried, and served in a sauce containing Barolo red wine.

alla **Bismark:** Fried, served topped with a fried egg.

alla **Bordolese:** Fried in butter and served in a rich red wine sauce containing beef marrow.

al **Cognac:** Fried in butter and served in a sauce of ham, mushrooms in which cognac has been flamed.

al **Madera:** Fried in butter with Madeira wine, served in a sauce made of pan juices and additional wine.

TRIPPE (A): Tripe; the stomach lining of veal or beef.

alla **Bolognese:** Beef tripe cut into strips and braised or stewed in lard, onion, garlic, parsley, and served with egg yolk and grated Parmesan cheese poured over it, then placed under the broiler.

TRIPPE: (cont.)

    alla **Fiorentina:** Florence style; veal tripe and veal foot stewed in herbal tomato sauce, with onion, and grated Parmesan cheese on top.

    alla **Milanese:** Milan style (Busecca); strips stewed in a sauce of onion, carrot, butter, pork fat, and tomatoes. Later cabbage, dried white beans, and potatoes are added with sage leaf, saffron, garlic and some parsley. Finally grated Parmesan cheese is put on top just before serving.

    Nostrana: As done in the house or restaurant; their own recipe.

    alla **Romana:** Roman style; strips served in a tomato sauce with herbs, mint leaves, and grated Pecorino (sharp cheese made of ewe's milk) on top.

    in **Umido:** Braised in a stew with tomatoes and herbs.

TRITATA: Ground as in hamburger.

VALDOSTANA: A veal cutlet or scaloppina, done in style of Valley of Aosta. Is classically either stuffed with a slice of Fontina cheese, breaded, and fried golden; or the cutlet, breaded and fried golden, then put under broiler with slice of Fontina cheese over it to melt it.

    dello **Chef:** Same as above with chef's own twist added.

    con **Tartufi:** Same but with a slice of white truffle placed on the cheese.

VALIGETTA: Literally a suitcase, but is a stuffed, braised or roasted veal breast roll.

VENTRESCA e FAGIOLI: Boiled pork paunch (the part bacon is made of) served with boiled dry white beans, usually eaten cold.

VITELLO: Veal; the most important meat in Italy. Where a meat dish is frequently given on the menu by the name of the cut (for instance: SCALOPPINI is many times simply called Scaloppini instead of Scaloppini di Vitello), you will find it separately listed in its alphabetical place in this section.

    Arrosto: Veal loin or leg roast.

    Arrosto al Soave: Roasted, bathed in Soave white wine.

    Asce di, ai Ferri: Grilled veal hamburger.

    Battuta di: A thin veal cutlet, same as Paillard. Or, could also be ground.

    Bianchette di: A veal stew in rich white cream sauce with herbs and mushrooms.

    Bistecca di: Grilled or braised loin veal steak.

VITELLO: (cont.)

Brasato di, al Barolo: Veal pot-roast marinated in, and braised in Barolo red wine with herbs, butter, ham fat.

Coda di, al Forno: Calf tail braised, and roasted in the oven.

Controfiletto di, ai Ferri: Loin steak of veal grilled or broiled.

Contronoce al Forno: Roast bottom round of veal.

Contronoce alla Genovese: Bottom round, Genoa style; a pot-roast braised in chopped vegetables, red wine, dried mushrooms, ham, and broth. May use white instead of red wine.

Coscia di, al Forno: Roast leg of veal.

Costata di: Veal loin chop.

Costola: Chest ribs of veal, roasted or broiled.

Costoletta (e) di: Veal rib chop or steak; (See under Costa, etc.).

Cotoletta: A veal steak without bone (See under Cotoletta).

Fegato di: Veal liver, see under Fegato.

Fettini di: Meaning slices or cutlets; alla Pizzaiola is served fried, in a sauce of garlic, oil, tomato, oregano and pan juices.

Filetto di, alla Rossini: Tenderloin steak of veal fried in butter and served on butter-fried bread, slices of foie gras (goose liver) on top; a slice of truffle on top of that, then sprinkled with a few drops of Madeira wine.

al **Forno:** Roast veal.

Frittura Piccata: Slices of veal in batter, or breaded and deep-fried.

con **Funghi:** Pieces of veal cooked one way or another and served with mushrooms.

Girello di: Lengthwise ligament of round steak of leg of veal, roasted whole or sliced and fried.

Lingua di: Calf tongue, usually boiled, or may be pickled or corned.

Lombata di: Loin of veal. May be a steak or a roast from that area.

Magro di: Lean veal meat, usually slices from loin or leg.

Muscoletti di, con Funghi: Lower shank including hock and knuckle pieces braised in white wine, rosemary, tomato, garlic, bay leaf, cloves, combined with cooked mushrooms and meat sauce. A sort of thick stew or ragout.

VITELLO: (cont.)

Noce di: Sirloin of veal, either roasted or grilled in slices. Could also be round steak cut.

Piccata di: Small-sized veal cutlets (See under Piccata).

Portafoglio: A thin veal cutlet usually stuffed (See under Portafoglio).

Punta di, al Forno Ripiene: Roast brisket or breast of veal with a stuffing of ground meat and herbs.

Punta di Petto: Same as Punta above - - the point of the breast.

Rollatine di: Rolled stuffed; roasted, or braised breast of veal (See under Rollatine).

Scaloppine (di): (See under Scaloppine).

Scanello di, Glassato: Round steak ligament of veal stripped out lengthwise and roasted or braised with onions, and cooked basted with vinegar, and sugar-glazed.

Sottonoce di: Another cut from the round of the leg of veal.

Spalla di, al Forno: Roast shoulder of veal.

Spezzato di: Veal stew; pieces braised in some herbal tomato gravy with wine, or can be a pot roast in same type of gravy.

Svizzerina di: Veal hamburger (ground), usually from shank.

Tenneroni di, con Piselli: Tenderloin of veal braised in Marsala wine, broth, bay leaf, ham fat, with peas put in at end of cooking.

Testina di: Calf's head, de-boned and brewed in aromatic broth.

Tonnato: Served cold. Usually a rolled veal roast braised or pot-roasted in white wine, herbs, lemon juice, oil and water. Then sliced, and covered with a thick mayonnaise sauce containing mashed canned tuna and anchovies, lemon juice, cream and stock, garnished with capers, lemon slices, and black olives.

Trancia di: Slice of veal.

ai **Funghi:** Slices of veal fried and served in a sauce with mushrooms.

all'**Uccelletto:** Literally meaning « a la little wild birds », but is only veal cutlets sautéed in oil and butter, with fresh sage leaves on each slice. The flavor imparted by the sage recalls the flavor of wild birds. Recent cooking practices also use this same term for cutlets prepared with bay leaf and garlic instead of the sage.

VITELLO: (cont.)

Vitellini con Funghi: Implying even younger, tinier veal cutlets braised in onion, herbs, tomato paste sauce with mushrooms.

Vitelluccia da Latte: Another diminutive name for milk-fed veal.

WURSTEL con Crauti: Fankfurters (hot dogs), boiled and served with sauerkraut.

ZAMPA: Boiled beef feet (as with pig's feet) served in some aromatic sauce.

ZAMPONE: Stuffed pig's foot sausage -- a pig's foot skin emptied of meat and bone, then stuffed back into original shape with sausage of its meat mixed with spices and herbs. Often served with zucchini squash or spinach after being boiled, or with cooked lentils.

CACCIAGIONE, SELVAGGINA
(Wild Game, Including Birds)

Wild game and fowl are regional and seasonal dishes in Italy, but will be found on menus in many different areas when they are available. The animals and birds are sold not only to restaurants, but also in the open markets, and shops.

There are four types of venison: CAMOSCIO (chamois), their smallest specie of deer; CAPRIOLO (roebuck), another small specie of deer; CERVO, a very large antlered deer; and DAINO, another very large antlered deer.

Other frequently served game include CINGHIALE (wild boar), CONIGLIO (rabbit), and LEPRE (hare).

Wild birds offered are ANITRA (duck), BECCACCIA (woodcock), BECCACCINO (snipe), FAGIANO (pheasant), PERNICE (partridge), PICCIONE SELVATICO (wild pigeon), QUAGLIA (quail), and a great variety of small song birds (thrushes, larks, ortolans), called TORDI or UCCELLETTI.

Methods of cooking venison or rabbit will be stews, with the meat usually being marinated before cooking, or for steaks to be grilled, and larger cuts roasted or spit-roasted. A well-known and frequently employed preparation for all types of wild game dishes is alla CACCIATORA (hunter's style), the meat braised in a sauce with such herbs as sage, rosemary, oregano, often with mushrooms and other vegetables and with wine added.

Small birds are usually cooked in a casserole with wine and seasonings, or skewered and roasted on a spit or in the oven, and flavored with sage or other herbs. The larger birds can be stuffed with dry fruit such as prunes or apricots, cooked chestnuts or herbs.

Game dishes are often served on a bed of seasoned rice, RISOTTO, or on POLENTA (a thick cornmeal mush mixture), or CROSTINI or CROSTONE, toasted or fried rounds of bread, small or large.

CACCIAGIONE, SELVAGGINA
(Wild Game Including Birds)

ALLODOLE: Larks.

ANITRA GERMANO: Mallard duck.

ANITRA SELVATICA: Wild duck.

all'**Arancia:** Roasted in the oven and served with a sauce made of pan juices, orange juice and finely shredded orange peel, garnished with quartered or sliced oranges.

ANITROCCOLO: Duckling.

ARROSTO: Roasted.

BECCACCIA: Woodcock.

BECCACCINO: Snipe.

al **Sugo Piccante:** Cooked in a seasoned brown sauce.

BECCAFICO: Warbler, a song bird.

CACCIATORA (alla): Hunter's style - - The game is braised in a sauce which normally includes as seasoning sage, rosemary, olive oil, wine, vinegar, and has in it garlic, tomatoes, carrots, onions and mushrooms.

CAMOSCIO: Chamois, their smallest specie of deer.

CAPRIOLO: Roebuck, a small specie of deer.

alla **Casalinga con Polenta:** Braised in a homemade style stew, and served with Polenta.

CARTOCCIO (al): Roasted in a paper bag or other such sealed covering.

CERVO: A very large antlered deer.

CINGHIALE: Wild boar, actually, wild pig, boar or sow.

Bistecca di: Loin or leg steak.

Lonza di: Loin.

CONIGLIO SELVATICO: Wild rabbit.

CRETA (in): Roasted in a clay casing.

CROSTINI (ONE): Toasted or fried rounds of bread, small or large.

DAINO: A very large antlered deer.

Cosciotto di: Upper leg of venison.

Sella di: Saddle of venison.

FAGIANELLA: Bustard, a running desert bird between the size of a large grouse and a small turkey, depending upon the variety.

FAGIANO: Pheasant, usually roasted in one way or another, and can be stuffed, with dry fruits or herbs, or flavored with sage, oregano, rosemary or other herbs.

FARAONA: Guinea fowl.

all'**Arancia:** Same as Anitra Selvatica all'Arancia.

Lardarellata alla Fiamma: Larded and cooked over open fire, as over charcoal.

FARCITO: Stuffed, usually with dry prunes or apricots, chestnuts or herbs.

FORNO (al): Roasted in the oven.

GRIGLIA (alla): Grilled.

LEPRE: Hare, a jack-rabbit size rabbit.

in **Salmi:** Jugged hare, or stew of marinated hare.

OLIVE (con): With olives.

PAGNOTTA del CACCIATORE: Game birds individually encased in bread dough and baked in the oven until the dough becomes crusty.

PALOMBACCIO: Wild pigeon.

PERNICE: Partridge.

PICCIONE SELVATICO: Wild pigeon.

POLENTA: A thick cornmeal mush mixture which is a very common accompaniment for game dishes.

QUAGLIE: Quail. These birds are raised domestically.

  in **Casseruola con Funghi:** Cooked in a casserole with mushrooms and herbs in a sauce.

  al **Crostone di Polenta:** Roasted and served on a round base of Polenta.

  al **Mattone:** Roasted in a brick oven.

  alla **Montanara:** Cooked in a red wine sauce.

  con **Piselli:** Roasted, served with peas cooked with onions, chopped ham, herbs.

RISOTTO: Rice. Roasted game birds are often served on a bed of well-seasoned rice.

SPIEDO (allo): Skewered and roasted, or roasted on a spit.

STAGIONATA: Well-aged or hung.

STARNA: Grey partridge.

SUGO: Sauce.

TORDO (I): Thrush.

UCCELLI (ETTI): Any number of small song birds such as thrushes, ortolans, larks, warblers.

CONTORNI, LEGUMI, VERDURE
(Vegetables)

In Italy, careful cultivation, without the over use of chemicals, results in the production of a large variety of vegetables, usually of superior quality. Their freshness and flavor is highlighted by the fact that they are normally served at the height of their season.

Raw vegetables such as POMODORI (tomatoes), RADICI (radishes), PEPERONI (bell peppers), CETRIOLI (cucumbers), are served as part of an ANTIPASTO (appetizer) course. Also as a first course, as well as an accompaniment to a main course, you will find cold, cooked vegetables such as FAGIOLINI (string beans), SPINACI (spinach), ZUCCHINI (Italian squash), ASPARAGI (asparagus).

Since hot, or cold cooked vegetables are a course in a meal, they are listed separately on the menu, and served on a separate plate. They can be FRITTO (deep-fried), al FORNO (baked), FARCITO or RIPIENO (stuffed), BOLLITO or LESSATO (boiled), SALTATE (sautéed), STUFATO (braised), or even alla GRIGLIA (grilled).

INSALATA VERDE (green salad) can consist of one or a combination of various types of LATTUGA (lettuce), and is served after the main course.

There are standard preparations offered over and over again for many different vegetables both raw and cooked. For raw, and cold cooked vegetables all'AGRO (with oil and lemon juice or vinegar), all'OLIO (oil), con MAIONESE (mayonnaise); and for hot cooked vegetables BOLLITI or LESSATI (boiled), al BURRO (with butter), FRITTI (deep-fried), al GRATIN (with or without a cream sauce, bread crumbs or grated cheese or both, and browned in the oven). These are listed alphabetically in this section, and not repeated under a given vegetable unless the preparation is somewhat special.

CONTORNI, LEGUMI, VERDURE
(Vegetables)

ACETO: Vinegar.

   sott'**Aceto:** Preserved in vinegar.

AGLIO: Garlic.

AGRO (all'): A dressing of olive oil and lemon juice or vinegar.

AGRODOLCE: A sweet-sour sauce.

ARROSTO (I): Roasted.

ASPARAGI: Asparagus (green).

    alla **Bismark:** Boiled, dressed with melted butter, and topped with a fried egg.

    alla **Milanese:** Boiled, served with melted butter, grated Parmesan cheese, and topped with a fried egg.

    alla **Parmigiana:** Boiled, served with melted butter and grated Parmesan cheese.

    all'**Uovo:** Same as alla Milanese.

BARBABIETOLE, BARBE ROSSE: Red beets.

BASILICO: Basil. This herb is used to flavor all types of dishes.

BESCIAMELLA (alla): The same thickened white sauce that we use on certain vegetables, made with butter, flour and milk.

BIETOLE (INI): Swiss chard.

    alla **Padella:** Cooked in a frying pan with butter or oil.

BOLLITO (I): Boiled.

BRASATO (I): Braised.

BROCCOLI (ETTI): Broccoli.

    al **Prosciutto:** Boiled, sautéed with chopped ham.

    alla **Romana:** Cooked in olive oil, garlic and white wine.

BURRO (al): Cooked vegetables tossed in melted butter in a frying pan.

CALDO (A): Warm or hot.

CAPONATA: Fried eggplant, onions, tomatoes, peppers, zucchini mixed together, and seasoned with capers, olives, vinegar and sugar. May be garnished with various seafoods. Served cold.

CAPONATINA: Same as above but more simple preparation.

CARCIOFI: Artichokes.

    Carciofini: Very small tender artichokes or the hearts of artichokes.

    Cuori di: Artichoke hearts.

    Fondi di: Artichoke bottoms.

    Fritti: Center part of the artichoke is quartered, dipped in a batter and deep-fried.

    alla **Giudia:** Tender, specially trimmed whole artichokes deep-fried in oil and then flattened out to resemble a rose.

    in **Pinzimonio:** Raw, tender artichokes eaten with an oil-based dressing.

CARCIOFI: (cont.)

alla **Romana (Romanesca):** Whole tender artichokes stuffed with mint leaves, garlic, parsley, cooked in olive oil and white wine.

CARDI: Cardoons - - stalks of an artichoke-type plant.

alla **Perugina:** Cut in pieces, boiled, then dipped in a batter and deep-fried.

CAROTE: Carrots.

Vichy: Cooked in butter and Vichy water, glazed with sugar.

CASTAGNE: Chestnuts.

CATALOGNA: A long-leafed salad green.

CAVOLETTI, CAVOLI (INI) di BRUXELLES: Brussels sprouts.

CAVOLFIORI: Cauliflower.

alla **Besciamella:** Boiled, served with a creamed white sauce, sprinkled with a mixture of grated Parmesan and bread crumbs, and browned in the oven.

CAVOLO ROSSO: Red cabbage.

CAVOLO VERDE: Green cabbage.

Involtini di: Meat-stuffed cabbage leaves, rolled and cooked in a sauce.

CECI: Chick peas or garbanzo beans.

CETRIOLI: Cucumbers.

CICORIA: Wild chicory, which is also now cultivated. A green or red-leafed type of lettuce with a slightly bitter taste, eaten in salads and also cooked.

del **Campo:** Wild chicory.

CIPOLLE: Onions.

Ripiene: Stuffed with a bread and chopped meat mixture flavored with herbs, and baked in the oven.

CIPOLLINE: Little white onions.

all'**Agrodolce:** In a sweet and sour tomato sauce.

Glassate: Glazed in broth with seasonings.

Novelli: Green onions or scallions.

al **Pomodoro:** Stewed with tomatoes, or in a tomato sauce.

COTTO (A): Cooked.

CRAUTI: Sauerkraut (pickled cabbage).

CRUDO: Raw.

ERBETTE: Cooked Swiss chard or other tender greens.

FAGIOLI: Dried or fresh beans of all types.

Bianchi: White.

con le **Cotiche:** Beans cooked in thick tomato sauce with slices of pork rind.

FAGIOLI: (cont.)

>>**Cotti al Forno:** Baked beans.

>alla **Fiorentina:** White beans boiled with salt and pepper, then olive oil added.

>>**Freschi al Pomodoro:** Fresh beans cooked with tomatoes, onions, diced ham.

>>**Lessati al Forno:** Boiled beans baked in the oven.

>all'**Olio:** Same as alla Fiorentina.

>>**Rossi:** Red kidney beans.

>>**Sgranati Freschi:** Fresh shelled beans boiled.

>>>**Lessi:** Same as above.

>>**Toscani:** White beans cooked with olive oil, garlic, sage.

>all'**Uccelletto:** Boiled white beans in a sauce of tomato, sage, garlic.

FAGIOLINI: String beans.

FARCITO (I): Stuffed or filled.

FAVE: Broad beans.

>al **Guanciale:** Cooked with onions and diced fat bacon.

FINOCCHIO: Fennel, a white, celery-like vegetable with a licorice flavor.

>alla **Parmigiana:** Gratineed with butter and Parmesan cheese.

>in **Pinzimonio:** Raw, dipped in an olive oil dressing.

FORNO (al): Baked in the oven.

FREDDO (A): Cold.

FRESCO (A): Fresh.

FRITTO (I): Deep-fried with or without a batter.

FUNGHI (ETTI) (ETTINI): Mushrooms of different sizes, both wild and cultivated.

>>**Fritti:** Dipped in batter and deep-fried.

>al **Funghetto:** Sliced, cooked in oil, garlic, herbs.

>alla **Griglia:** Grilled.

>>**Porcini:** A variety of wild mushroom (Boletus).

>>**Trifolati:** Sliced, cooked in butter and oil, garlic, anchovies, lemon juice.

GIARDINIERA: A garnish of cooked or preserved vegetables cut in small pieces.

GRATIN (al), GRATINATE: Cooked and served with or without a white cream sauce, sprinkled with bread crumbs or grated cheese or both, and browned in the oven.

GRIGLIA (alla): Grilled.

INDIVIA: Endive or curly-leafed lettuce.

>>**Belga:** Belgian endive - - a small, elongated head with crispy, whitish leaves, eaten in salads, also braised.

INSALATA: Salad. These are made of various raw and cooked vegetables or different combinations of them, and usually served with an oil and vinegar dressing. To find the principal ingredient of a salad as INSALATA di POMODORI, see under POMODORI (tomatoes).

   di **Campo:** Field lettuce.

     Capricciosa: Raw vegetables such as bell peppers, cucumbers, tomatoes, celery, and may include diced ham or sausage, cut in small pieces with an oil and vinegar dressing, or, with mayonnaise when served as an ANTI-PASTO (appetizer).

     Composta Cotta: Mixture of cold cooked vegetables.

     Cotta: Cold cooked vegetable salad.

   di **Crudita:** Mixed raw vegetables.

     Mista: Mixed or combination salad.

     Verde: Tossed green salad with oil and vinegar dressing.

LATTUGA: Lettuce.

   Romana: Romaine.

LENTICCHIE: Lentils.

LESSATO (I): Boiled.

LIMONE (al): With lemon juice.

MACEDONIA DI LEGUMI: Mixture of cooked vegetables.

MAIONESE (con): With mayonnaise.

MARINATO (I): Marinated.

MELANZANE: Eggplant.

   ai **Ferri:** Sliced and grilled.

   alla **Fiorentina:** Cooked in alternating layers with cheese and tomatoes.

   al **Funghetto:** Chopped, stewed in oil, garlic, herbs, tomato sauce.

     Gratinate: Split lengthwise, fried in oil, pulp mixed with other ingredients, put back in shell, sprinkled with bread crumbs and grated Parmesan cheese and browned in the oven.

   alla **Napoletana:** Sliced, fried, put in baking dish, layered with tomato sauce, slices of Mozzarella cheese and grated Parmesan cheese and baked in the oven.

   alla **Parmigiana:** Same as above.

MISTO (A) (I): Mixed.

NAVONI: Yellow Turnips.

NOSTRALE (NOSTRANO): Home product, home-grown or local.

OLIO: Oil, usually olive oil.

    all'**Olio:** With olive oil and salt and pepper.

    sott'**Olio:** Preserved in oil.

OLIVE: Olives.

    Nere: Black.

    Verde: Green.

PASSATO: Puree.

    di **Lenticchie:** Of lentils.

    di **Marroni:** Of chestnuts.

    di **Patate:** Mashed potatoes.

    di **Piselli Secchi:** Of cooked dried split peas.

PATATE: Potatoes.

    Arrosto: Peeled, roasted, whole or cut into various shapes.

    Crocchette di: Croquettes.

    al **Forno:** Baked with the skin on.

    Fritte: French-fried potatoes.

    all'**Ghiotto:** Baked stuffed.

    Saltate: Sautéed - - boiled, sliced, then fried in butter.

PATATINE NOVELLE: New potatoes.

    al **Forno:** Baked with the skin on.

    alla **Paesana:** Sliced raw, seasoned with herbs, and baked in stock in the oven.

PEPE: Pepper.

PEPERONATA: Sliced bell peppers, onions, tomatoes, stewed in oil and garlic, and served cold.

PEPERONCINI: A small conical green pepper preserved in vinegar.

PEPERONI: Bell peppers (red, yellow and green).

    al **Gratin:** Sliced, put in a casserole with oil, seasoned with capers, anchovies, sprinkled with bread crumbs and grated cheese, and baked in the oven.

    in **Padella:** Cooked in a frying pan, often with onions, tomatoes, herbs.

    Ripieni: Stuffed with various fillings, such as rice and chopped meat, and baked in the oven.

PINZIMONIO (in): An oil, salt and pepper dressing for certain raw vegetables.

PISELLI: Peas.

    alla **Fiorentina:** Mixed with chopped ham, onions, herbs, tomato sauce.

    al **Guanciale:** Cooked with chopped onions and diced fat bacon.

    Novelli: Fresh, tender.

CONTORNI

PISELLI: (cont.)

al **Prosciutto:** Sautéed with prosciutto (ham) and onions.

alla **Toscana:** Same as alla Fiorentina.

al **Uccelletto:** Cooked in a tomato sauce flavored with sage.

POMODORI: Tomatoes.

al **Forno:** Halves of tomatoes flavored with herbs, garlic, grated cheese, and baked in the oven.

al **Gratin, Gratinati:** Cut in thick slices, put in oiled baking pan, covered with bread crumbs and grated cheese, and baked in the oven.

Ripieni: Stuffed with a filling of such ingredients as sautéed onions, chopped herbs, bread crumbs, and baked in the oven.

PORRI: Leeks.

alla **Crema:** In a cream sauce.

Dorate: Dipped in a batter and deep-fried.

PREZZEMOLO: Parsley.

PUREA, PURE: Pureed (mashed or put through a sieve).

di **Patate:** Mashed potatoes.

RADICCHIO: Wild chicory, which is also now cultivated. A narrow green or red-leafed type of lettuce with a slightly bitter taste, eaten in salads and also cooked. Barba di Cappuccino or Trevisano (red-leafed), Verde (green-leafed).

RADICI, RAPANELLI, RAVANELLI: Red radishes.

RAPE: Turnips.

Broccoletti di, Cime di: Turnip greens.

Rosse: White turnips, with rose coloration.

RIPIENE (I): Stuffed or filled.

SALE: Salt.

SALTATE: Sauteed.

SCAROLA: Escarole, a crispy-leafed, bunch lettuce.

SEDANO: Celery.

SFORMATO: Like a souffle - - a preparation with eggs and pureed cooked vegetables baked in a mold in the oven.

SOTTOACETI: Various vegetables pickled in vinegar. Also means pickles.

SPINACI: Spinach.

al **Burro e Parmigiano:** Cooked spinach seasoned with butter and grated Parmesan cheese.

al **Gratin:** Cooked spinach mixed with butter, salt and pepper, topped with grated Parmesan cheese and re-heated in the oven.

SPINACI: (cont.)

   alla **Parmigiana:** Same as al Burro e Parmigiano.

STAGIONE (di): In season.

STUFATO (I): Braised, stewed.

TARTUFI: Truffles, aromatic fungus which grow wild underground, and are considered a delicacy.

      Bianchi: White.

      Neri: Black.

TEGAME, TEGAMINO (al): Sauteed in butter or oil in a small, individual frying pan with two loop handles, in which the vegetables are also served.

UMIDO (in): Braised or stewed.

VERDURE COTTE: Cooked vegetables.

VERZA: Savoy or crinkly-leafed cabbage.

ZUCCHINI: Italian squash.

   in **Carpione:** Marinated, served cold.

      Farciti: Filled with a mixture of chopped ham, mushrooms, herbs, grated cheese, bread crumbs, and baked in the oven.

      Fritti: Dipped in batter and deep-fried.

   al **Gratin:** Baked in the oven with a white sauce, various seasonings, and topped with bread crumbs and grated Parmesan cheese.

      Parmigiana di Zucchini: Cooked and served with melted butter and grated Parmesan cheese.

      Scapecce: Cut in pieces, fried in oil with garlic, mint, vinegar.

      Trifolati: Sliced, cooked in butter, garlic, lemon juice, parsley.

ZUCCA: A large yellow squash similar to a pumpkin but oblong.

      Fiori di, Ripiene: Large, bright yellow squash flowers stuffed and served with a sauce.

DOLCI, GELATI, FRUTTA
(Sweets or Desserts, Ice Creams, Fruit)

DOLCI (desserts) and GELATI (ice creams) can be listed separately or together on the menu, or sometimes under the general heading of FRUTTA (fruit), for fruit is considered a dessert, whether eaten plain, or with PANNA (whipped cream), ice cream, or flavored with wine, liqueur or fruit juice.

Under DOLCI you will find many different kinds of TORTA (a type of rich cake), CROSTATA (an open-faced fruit pie), and PASTICCERIA ASSORTITA (assorted pastries) served al CARRELLO (from the food cart).

GELATI will include ice cream and sherbert of all flavors served plain or with fruit, whipped cream or a sauce, and frozen, molded desserts known as SEMIFREDDI (half-cold) which contain combinations of ice cream, custard, whipped cream, candied fruits and nuts.

Rich and elaborate desserts are served on festive occasions, but in general pastries and ice cream dishes are more often eaten between meals at outdoor cafes or bars, the Italians preferring fruit in some form as their dessert.

FRUTTA (fruit) is usually brought to the table in a CESTINO di FRUTTA (large basket) from which you take your choice (A SCELTA, A PIACERE), and are charged accordingly. The basket will be filled with whole fruit in season (Di STAGIONE) as ARANCI (oranges), CILIEGE (cherries), ALBICOCCHE (apricots), MELE (apples), PERE (pears), PRUGNE (plums), UVA (grapes).

MACEDONIA di FRUTTA (fresh fruit salad), FRAGOLE (strawberries) and LAMPONI (raspberries) often have a dry or sweet wine or a liqueur poured over them, or can be served topped with ice cream or whipped cream.

Some famous Italian desserts are CASSATA and SPUMONI (both molded ice cream desserts), ZABAGLIONE (a wine-flavored custard), and ZUPPA INGLESE (English soup), which is not a soup at all, but an elaborate version of the English trifle, a kind of pudding cake.

DOLCI, GELATI, FRUTTA
(Sweets or Desserts, Ice Creams, Fruit)

AFFETTATO (I): Sliced.

ALBICOCCHE: Apricots.

AMARETTI: Macaroons.

ANANAS, ANANASSO: Pineapple.

ARACHIDE: Peanuts.

ARANCI: Oranges.

ARANCIA (al): With orange juice.

ASSORTITI (E): Assorted.

AVELLANE: Hazelnuts.

BANANE: Bananas.

BISCOTTI: Cookies.

BISCUIT TORTONI: A frozen dessert of beaten egg whites, whipped cream and macaroon crumbs, topped with chopped toasted almonds.

BUDINO: Pudding.

CAFFE (al): With coffee flavoring.

CALDO (A): Warm, or hot.

CANDITA: Candied.

CANNOLI: Cylindrical pastry cases filled with sweetened RICOTTA cheese, mixed with cocoa and candied fruits.

CARRELLO (al) (servizio al): Served from the food cart.

CASA (della): Of the restaurant.

CASALINGA (alla): Homemade style.

CASSATA GELATA: A dome-shaped mold containing various flavors of ice cream, candied fruits and nuts, served in wedges.

CASSATA alla SICILIANA: A layered cake made with PAN di SPAGNA (a sponge cake) lightly dipped in Marsala wine, and spread with a cream of RICOTTA cheese, containing sugar, chocolate and candied fruits. Can be served plain, or with whipped cream or meringue topping.

CASTAGNACCIO: A dessert made of chestnut flour paste with pine nuts, almonds, raisins, candied fruits, and baked until crusty. Served cold.

CASTAGNE: Chestnuts.

CESTINO di FRUTTA: A basket of fruit.

CIALDE: Wafers.

CILIEGE: Cherries.

CIOCCOLATA: Chocolate, or chocolate-flavored.

COCOMERO: Watermelon.

COMPOSTA di FRUTTA: Compote, or stewed fruit.

COPPA: Cup or goblet - - a dessert dish.

COPPA GELATO: A dish of mixed flavors of ice cream.

COTTO: Cooked.

    al **Forno:** Baked in the oven.

CREMA (alla): With cream, or custard.

CREMA CARAMELLA: A custard with a caramelized sugar sauce on top.

CROSTATA: An open-faced pie with pastry base, filled with fruit, custard or other filling, and with various toppings. The ingredient which gives it its particular name, you can identify in this section in its alphabetical order. For example, to translate CROSTATA di FRAGOLE, look under FRAGOLE (strawberries).

DATTERO: Date.

DOLCI: Sweets or desserts.

FIAMMA (alla): Flamed, usually with brandy.

FICHI: Figs.

FLAMBÉ: Flamed, usually with brandy.

FRAGOLE: Strawberries.

FRAGOLINE di BOSCO: Very small, bright red wild strawberries.

FRAGOLONE: Very large cultivated strawberries.

FRESCO (A): Fresh.

FRUTTA: Fruit.

FUNDADOR (al): With Spanish Fundador brandy.

GELATO (l) (al): Ice Cream, or with ice cream.

    di **Tartufo:** With chocolate sauce poured over.

GHIACCIO: Ice.

GIORNO (del): Of the day.

GRANITA: Finely shaved ice with fruit syrups, as lemon, strawberry, cherry, or other flavorings poured over.

    di **Caffe con Panna:** Finely shaved ice with strong black coffee poured over, served in a parfait glass with alternating layers of whipped cream.

KIRSCH (al): With Kirsch, a clear cherry brandy.

LAMPONI: Raspberries.

LIMONE (al): With lemon juice, or lemon-flavored.

LIQUORE (al): With brandy or other liquor.

MACEDONIA di FRUTTA: Fruit salad.

MANDARINO: Tangerine.

MANDORLE, MANDORLATA: With almonds.

MANTECATO: A type of ice-cream with a frozen whipped cream texture.

MARASCHINO, MARASCO (al): With maraschino liqueur.
MARRONE: Large chestnut.
MARSALA (al): With Marsala, a fortified sweet wine.
MELACOTOGNA: Quince.
MELAGRANA: Pomegranate.
MELE: Apples.
    Renetta: A variety of apple.
MELONE: Melon.
    Cantalupo: Cantaloupe.
MENTA: Flavored with mint, or Creme de Menthe.
MERINGA: Meringue shells.
    Chantilly: Filled with whipped cream.
  con **Gelato:** Filled with ice cream.
MERINGATO: Meringue.
MIRABELLA: Small yellow plum.
MIRTILLI: Closely resemble blueberries or huckleberries.
MISTO (A) (I): Mixed.
MOKA: Flavored with mocha coffee.
MONTE BIANCO: Boiled, riced chestnuts, sweetened and formed into a pyramid shape, and covered with whipped cream to resemble Mont Blanc.
MORE: Mulberries.
NESPOLA: Medlar, a tart fruit which grows wild in Europe.
    di **Giappone:** Japanese medlar or loquat.
NOCCIOLE: Hazelnuts or filberts.
NOCCIOLINE AMERICANE: Peanuts.
NOCE: Walnut.
NOCE di COCCO: Coconut.
PAN di SPAGNA: Sponge cake, a base for many desserts.
PANDORO di VERONA: A very light cake made in a deep, star-shaped mold, and sprinkled with sugar.
PANETTONE: A dome-shaped cake-bread or coffeecake with raisins and candied fruits; made in all sizes.
PANFORTE: A flat, hard fruit cake with almonds, hazelnuts, honey, citron rind.
PANNA (alla) (con): With cream or whipped cream.
    Montata: Whipped cream.
PASTICCERIA: Pastry.
PASTICCINI da TE: Teacakes, petits fours, small pastries.
PERE: Pears.
PERE HELENE (ELENA): Pear, poached in vanilla-flavored syrup, served with vanilla ice cream, covered with warm chocolate sauce.

PESCA MELBA: Peach poached in syrup, served with vanilla ice cream, and raspberry sauce poured over.

PESCHE: Peaches.

PEZZO (a) (un): By the piece.

PIACERE (a): Of your choice.

PINOCCATE (PINOCCHIATA): A sweet made of beaten syrup and pine nuts; a specialty of Perugia.

PINOCCHIO, PINOLI: Pine nuts.

PISTACCHI: Pistachio nuts.

POMPELMO: Grapefruit.

PORTO (al): With port wine.

PROFITEROLE al CIOCCOLATA: Small filled cream puffs with melted chocolate poured over, and garnished with whipped cream.

PRUGNE: Plums.

RABARBARO: Rhubarb.

RIBES NERO: Black currants.

RIBES ROSSO: Red currants.

RICOTTA: A type of cottage cheese which is sweetened and flavored when used in desserts.

ST. HONORE: A round pastry shell which is filled with a custard cream, and encircled with small cream puffs dipped in a sugar syrup.

SAVARIN: A cake baked in a ring mold, and then soaked in rum or Kirsch-flavored syrup, the center filled with fruit, topped with whipped cream.

SCELTA (a): Of your choice.

SCIROPPO (al), SCIROPPATE: Cooked in syrup.

SECCA: Dried.

SEMIFREDDI: All desserts, mostly molded, which are made with a whipped cream, ice cream, custard or gelatine mixture base, or a combination of any of them, which are frozen or refrigerated before being served.

SFOGLIATELLI: Small pastry forms filled with whipped cream, custard, or creamed and sweetened RICOTTA cheese, and candied fruits.

SORBETTO: Sherbet.

al **Calvados:** Flavored with Calvados liquor, an apple brandy.

SPUMONI: A frozen molded dessert made with any combination of different flavored ice creams, and candied fruits.

al **Croccante:** With toasted almonds caramelized in sugar, and then crushed into very small pieces. This preparation is used both in desserts and also sprinkled on top of them.

STAGIONE (di): Of the season, or in season.

SUSINE: Plums.

TARTUFI di CIOCCOLATA: Little ball-shaped sweets made of a chocolate, coffee, and egg mixture, and hardened in the refrigerator.

TORTA (E): Fundamentally a cake, in the sense of not having a pastry shell which would then make it a pie. It is usually any combination of layers of cake, custard, fruit, whipped cream, with or without a frosting. The ingredient which gives it its particular name you can identify in this section in its alphabetical order. For example, to translate TORTA di MELE, look under MELE (apples).

    Gelata: Ice cream and other ingredients molded into a round cake form.

    Meringa: Large meringue pie shell filled with fruit, topped with whipped cream.

    Millefoglie: A Napoleon - - very thin layers of pastry in a rectangular form with custard filling, topped with a sugar frosting.

    Zuccotto: A round, dome-shaped mold of a cake made of liquor-soaked sponge cake, filled with whipped or ice cream, melted chocolate, and candied fruits.

TORTIGLIONE: Almond cakes.

TORTINA di MARMELLATA: Jam tart.

TRANCIO (al): By the piece, or slice.

UVA: Grapes.

    Passa, Passita: Raisins.

    Spina: Gooseberry.

VANIGLIA: Vanilla-flavored.

VARI: Varied, assorted.

VINO (al): With wine.

    Rosso: With red wine.

VISCIOLA: Wild cherry.

ZABAGLIONE (ZABAIONE): A custard dessert made of cooked beaten egg yolks, sugar, and flavored with white or Marsala wine, served either warm or cold.

ZUCCOTTO: Same as Torta Zuccotto.

    Cavour: Variation of this cake.

    alla **Fiorentina:** Same as Zuccotto.

ZUPPA INGLESE: « English soup » - - an elaborate version of the English trifle, made of layers of spongecake or ladyfingers dipped in Marsala wine, or a liquor such as rum, interspersed in layers with vanilla or chocolate cream filling, or both, and decorated with whipped cream or meringue and candied fruits.

FORMAGGI
(Cheeses)

Cheeses are offered as a separate course in a meal, immediately after the main course.

Most menus will list their cheeses as FORMAGGI ASSORTITI (assorted) or MISTI (mixed) and serve them from a large plate from which you make your own selection, A SCELTA (of your choice), A PIACERE (your pleasure), or AL CARRELLO (from the food cart). Thus you can easily sample cheeses with which you are not familiar, to determine your preferences.

The cheese tray or plate will contain a good selection including such cheeses as GORGONZOLA (a creamy, blue-type, milder than Roquefort), GROVIERA SVIZZERA (Swiss cheese), BEL PAESE (a mild, soft cheese), STRACCHINO (a soft, creamy white cheese), PROVOLONE (a smooth, tasty cheese), as well as various cheeses used extensively in cooking such as PARMIGIANO (a hard, tasty cheese made of cow's milk), PECORINO (a hard, sharp cheese made of sheep's milk), and FONTINA (a smooth, mild white cheese).

HOW TO USE THE PRACTICE ME

1. Most menus will list under each category various dishes offered; the categories being the order in which the food is eaten. **Antip** tizers, or First course) lead the list, and the mer **Dolci** (Desserts).

2. On the **Carta** (the menu), the soups, ric and other flour-made dishes are in the gene of **Minestre**. In this book you will find soups the **Minestre** section, and all the flour-made p ghetti, noodles, ravioli, etc.) in the **Pasta** se courses will be found under **Pesce** (fish).

3. The meat, or main dishes (**Piatti del Gior** you will find in the **PIATTI del GIORNO** se dishes are sometimes included in the Piatti so if you cannot find a dish in that section, be under **CACCIAGIONE** (Game), a separ category which follows directly after Zampone del Giorno section.

ANTIPASTI

Antipasti Assortiti	
Prosciutto Crudo di Parma	
Insalata di Pesce	
Funghi all'Olio	
Filetti di Acciughe al Burro	
Salmone Affumicato	
Carciofini	

MINESTRE

Tortellini in Brodo	
Pastina in Brodo	
Ravioli alla Casalinga	
Tagliatelle alla Bolognese	
Lasagne al Forno	
Spaghetti alla Napoletana	
Spaghetti alla Carbonara	
Zuppa di Verdura	
Gnocchi alla Piemontese	
Risotto alla Milanese	

LA C

UOVA

	LIRE
Frittata alla Casalinga	1500
Omelette al Prosciutto	2200
Omelette con Formaggio	2000
Uova Strapazzate al Pomodoro	1800

PESCE

Sogliole alla Mugnaia	7000
Filetti di Sogliola Fritti	6000
Gamberi Fritti	6500
Fritto Misto Mare	3500
Muscoli alla Marinara	3000
Trancia di Cernia a Piacere	4800
Storione alla Milanese	6500
Calamaretti Fritti	5000

PIATTI del GIORNO

Costoletta alla Milanese	6000
Arrosto di Vitello	6500
1/4 Pollo Arrosto o alla Griglia	3500
Fegato alla Veneziana	3500
Lingua di Bue	3000
Ossobuco al Vino Bianco	4000
Zampone di Modena con Spinaci	5500
Fesa di Vitello al Forno	4500
Vitello Tonnato	6000

PIATTI da FARSI

Pollo alla Diavola	5500
Scaloppine alla Valdostana	6500
Fegatini di Pollo al Burro e Salvia	3500
Cervella alla Finanziera	9000
Bistecca alla Fiorentina	11000
Rognone Trifolato	7000
Costoletta di Maiale alla Griglia	5500
Paillard di Vitello ai Ferri	3000

PRICES LISTED ON THE PRACTICE MENU ARE NOT

RTA

Pane e Coperto L.1000

ATTI da FARSI (cont.)

	LIRE
giano Arrosto	8500
pre in Salmi	8000

CONTORNI

tate Fritte	1500
selli al Prosciutto	3800
giolini al Burro	1600
salata Mista	1000
salata Verde	900
salata di Pomodoro	900
rote al Burro	800

FORMAGGI

rgonzola, Bel Paese, Groviera, Emmenthal, Par-
giano.

sortiti a Porzione	2000

FRUTTA

re, Mele, Banane, Ciliege, Uva, Arance

Stagione, un Pezzo.	1200
agole alla Panna o Marsala	3000
nanas al Maraschino	2200
acedonia di Frutta	2000

GELATI

ssata Gelata	1500
ppa Gelato	1500
occolato Gelato	1600

DOLCI

sticceria Assortita	2500
rta Gelata.	2000
ema Caramella	1500
rta alla Casalinga	2000

CTUAL ONES

TABLE OF CONTENTS

**PRICES LISTED IN THE TEXT AND ON THE
PRACTICE MENU ARE NOT ACTUAL ONES.**

LA CA

UOVA	LIRE
Frittata alla Casalinga	1500
Omelette al Prosciutto	2200
Omelette con Formaggio.	2000
Uova Strapazzate al Pomodoro	1800

PESCE

Sogliole alla Mugnaia	7000
Filetti di Sogliola Fritti	6000
Gamberi Fritti.	6500
Fritto Misto Mare	3500
Muscoli alla Marinara	3000
Trancia di Cernia a Piacere	4800
Storione alla Milanese	6500
Calamaretti Fritti	5000

PIATTI del GIORNO

Costoletta alla Milanese	6000
Arrosto di Vitello	6500
1/4 Pollo Arrosto o alla Griglia.	3500
Fegato alla Veneziana	3500
Lingua di Bue.	3000
Ossobuco al Vino Bianco	4000
Zampone di Modena con Spinaci	5500
Fesa di Vitello al Forno	4500
Vitello Tonnato	6000

PIATTI da FARSI

Pollo alla Diavola	5500
Scaloppine alla Valdostana	6500
Fegatini di Pollo al Burro e Salvia	3500
Cervella alla Finanziera	9000
Bistecca alla Fiorentina	11000
Rognone Trifolato	7000
Costoletta di Maiale alla Griglia	5500
Paillard di Vitello ai Ferri	3000

PRICES LISTED ON THE PRACTICE MENU ARE NOT

HOW TO USE THE PRACTICE MENU

1. Most menus will list under each category of food the various dishes offered; the categories being arranged in the order in which the food is eaten. **Antipasti** (Appetizers, or First course) lead the list, and the menu ends with **Dolci** (Desserts).

2. On the **Carta** (the menu), the soups, rice, spaghetti, and other flour-made dishes are in the general category of **Minestre.** In this book you will find soups and rice in the **Minestre** section, and all the flour-made products (spaghètti, noodles, ravioli, etc.) in the **Pasta** section. Fish courses will be found under **Pesce** (fish).

3. The meat, or main dishes (**Piatti del Giorno,** da **Farsi**) you will find in the **PIATTI del GIORNO** section. Game dishes are sometimes included in the Piatti del Giorno, so if you cannot find a dish in that section, then it must be under **CACCIAGIONE** (Game), a separate complete category which follows directly after Zampone in the Piatti del Giorno section.

ANTIPASTI

	LIRE
Antipasti Assortiti	3000
Prosciutto Crudo di Parma	3000
Insalata di Pesce	2500
Funghi all'Olio	3000
Filetti di Acciughe al Burro	1800
Salmone Affumicato	5000
Carciofini	2000

MINESTRE

Tortellini in Brodo	1800
Pastina in Brodo	1600
Ravioli alla Casalinga	2500
Tagliatelle alla Bolognese	2200
Lasagne al Forno	3000
Spaghetti alla Napoletana	2000
Spaghetti alla Carbonara	3000
Zuppa di Verdura	1600
Gnocchi alla Piemontese	2300
Risotto alla Milanese	2000

FORMAGGI
(Cheeses)

Cheeses are offered as a separate course in a meal, immediately after the main course.

Most menus will list their cheeses as FORMAGGI ASSORTITI (assorted) or MISTI (mixed) and serve them from a large plate from which you make your own selection, A SCELTA (of your choice), A PIACERE (your pleasure), or AL CARRELLO (from the food cart). Thus you can easily sample cheeses with which you are not familiar, to determine your preferences.

The cheese tray or plate will contain a good selection including such cheeses as GORGONZOLA (a creamy, blue-type, milder than Roquefort), GROVIERA SVIZZERA (Swiss cheese), BEL PAESE (a mild, soft cheese), STRACCHINO (a soft, creamy white cheese), PROVOLONE (a smooth, tasty cheese), as well as various cheeses used extensively in cooking such as PARMIGIANO (a hard, tasty cheese made of cow's milk), PECORINO (a hard, sharp cheese made of sheep's milk), and FONTINA (a smooth, mild white cheese).

STAGIONE (di): Of the season, or in season.

SUSINE: Plums.

TARTUFI di CIOCCOLATA: Little ball-shaped sweets made of a chocolate, coffee, and egg mixture, and hardened in the refrigerator.

TORTA (E): Fundamentally a cake, in the sense of not having a pastry shell which would then make it a pie. It is usually any combination of layers of cake, custard, fruit, whipped cream, with or without a frosting. The ingredient which gives it its particular name you can identify in this section in its alphabetical order. For example, to translate TORTA di MELE, look under MELE (apples).

   Gelata: Ice cream and other ingredients molded into a round cake form.

   Meringa: Large meringue pie shell filled with fruit, topped with whipped cream.

   Millefoglie: A Napoleon - - very thin layers of pastry in a rectangular form with custard filling, topped with a sugar frosting.

   Zuccotto: A round, dome-shaped mold of a cake made of liquor-soaked sponge cake, filled with whipped or ice cream, melted chocolate, and candied fruits.

TORTIGLIONE: Almond cakes.

TORTINA di MARMELLATA: Jam tart.

TRANCIO (al): By the piece, or slice.

UVA: Grapes.

   Passa, Passita: Raisins.

   Spina: Gooseberry.

VANIGLIA: Vanilla-flavored.

VARI: Varied, assorted.

VINO (al): With wine.

   Rosso: With red wine.

VISCIOLA: Wild cherry.

ZABAGLIONE (ZABAIONE): A custard dessert made of cooked beaten egg yolks, sugar, and flavored with white or Marsala wine, served either warm or cold.

ZUCCOTTO: Same as Torta Zuccotto.

   Cavour: Variation of this cake.

   alla **Fiorentina:** Same as Zuccotto.

ZUPPA INGLESE: « English soup » - - an elaborate version of the English trifle, made of layers of spongecake or ladyfingers dipped in Marsala wine, or a liquor such as rum, interspersed in layers with vanilla or chocolate cream filling, or both, and decorated with whipped cream or meringue and candied fruits.

DOLCI
FRUTTA